T0295640

Architecting Experience

A Conversion Science Handbook

Second Edition

Advances and Opportunities with Big Data and Analytics

Series Editor: Russell Walker *(Northwestern University, USA)*

Published:

Vol. 3:   *Architecting Experience: A Conversion Science Handbook*
          Second Edition
          by Scot R. Wheeler

Vol. 2:   *Future Automation: Changes to Lives and to Businesses*
          by Timothy E. Carone

Vol. 1:   *Architecting Experience: A Marketing Science and*
          Digital Analytics Handbook
          by Scot R. Wheeler

Advances and Opportunities with Big Data and Analytics

Architecting Experience
A Conversion Science Handbook

Second Edition

Scot R Wheeler

Medill-Northwestern University, USA

 **World Scientific**

W JERSEY · LONDON · SINGAPORE · BEIJING · SHANGHAI · HONG KONG · TAIPEI · CHENNAI · TOKYO

Published by

World Scientific Publishing Co. Pte. Ltd.

5 Toh Tuck Link, Singapore 596224

USA office: 27 Warren Street, Suite 401-402, Hackensack, NJ 07601

UK office: 57 Shelton Street, Covent Garden, London WC2H 9HE

Library of Congress Cataloging-in-Publication Data
Names: Wheeler, Scot R, author.
Title: Architecting experience : a conversion science handbook / Scot R Wheeler.
Description: Second Edition. | USA : World Scientific, 2020. |
   Series: Advances and opportunities with big data and analytics |
   Revised edition of the author's Architecting experience, [2016]
Identifiers: LCCN 2020020088 | ISBN 9789811219863 (hardcover) |
   ISBN 9789811220104 (paperback) | ISBN 9789811219870 (ebook) |
   ISBN 9789811219887 (ebook other)
Subjects: LCSH: Communication in marketing. | Digital media.
Classification: LCC HF5415.123 .W48 2020 | DDC 658.8/02--dc23
LC record available at https://lccn.loc.gov/2020020088

British Library Cataloguing-in-Publication Data
A catalogue record for this book is available from the British Library.

For any available supplementary material, please visit
https://www.worldscientific.com/worldscibooks/10.1142/11816#t=suppl

Desk Editors: Balamurugan Rajendran/Sylvia Koh

Typeset by Stallion Press
Email: enquiries@stallionpress.com

Contents

About the Author ix

Introduction xi

Chapter ONE | **Content Creates Consumer Experience** 1

1.1 Experiencing Content 4
1.2 Conversion Science 19

Chapter TWO | **Media Moves Markets** 25

2.1 Media Product Conversion 25
2.2 Business to Consumer Conversion 26
2.3 Business to Business Conversion 26
2.4 Creating Attention and Action 27

Chapter THREE | **Data is the "New Oil": Analytics are Advanced Chemistry** 45

3.1 The Challenge to "Collect and Connect" 45

v

Chapter | **The Rush is on: Planning to Collect**
FOUR | **and Connect** | **71**

4.1 Applied Conversion Analytics Playbook | 71
4.2 ACAP Section One: Problem Definition | 72
4.3 ACAP Section Two: Consumer-centered
Solutions | 74

Chapter | **Consumer Attention: The Brass Ring**
FIVE | **on the Media-Go-Round** | **97**

5.1 Salience: Earning Attention | 98
5.2 Resonance: Building Memory | 118

Chapter | **To Mediate Should Mean to Motivate** | **125**
SIX
6.1 Media Strategy | 126
6.2 Tactical Plan | 128

Chapter | **Content and Experience Makes or**
SEVEN | **Breaks Conversion** | **153**

7.1 Search Engine Optimization, Search
Engine Marketing, and Organic
Social Media | 154
7.2 Voice Activated/Digital Assistants | 159
7.3 Web User Interface and User
Experience Design | 161
7.4 Applications | 167
7.5 Shopper Marketing | 168
7.6 E-Commerce | 169

Chapter EIGHT	**It's Never Good Enough**	**173**
	8.1 ACAP Section Three: Testing	173
	8.2 ACAP Section Three: Performance Measurement	183
	8.3 ACAP Section Three: Data Visualization	196

Chapter NINE	**Getting Ahead of the Game**	**203**
	9.1 ACAP Section 4: Data Management and Data Application	203
	9.2 Data Management	203
	9.3 Data Application: Predictive, Prescriptive, and Adaptive Analytics	215

Chapter TEN	**Content Creates Cultural Experience**	**225**
	10.1 The Information Society: Media Cycles and Feedback Loops	225
	10.2 Organizational Change for Effective Digital Analytics	247

Conclusion	261
Index	263

About the Author

 Scot Wheeler's leadership as an innovator, a manager and an educator in the integration of data-driven and science-based marketing, information technology and media kicked-off over 20 years ago. With an undergraduate degree in Sociology and Cultural Studies concentrated on media and consumer economics, it was his affinity for programming that started Scot's career in software development in the build-up to Y2K.

Scot's education in the cultural influence of media and his technical abilities were combined when he joined the pioneering efforts of a Web1.0 digital marketing agency. In the aftermath of the Web1.0 crash, Scot moved into enterprise BI and ERP analytics before being hired to help in a new pioneering field with the development of a social media listening technology start-up in 2007, where he led both product development and professional services.

Scot received his MBA in Strategy, Finance and Marketing from Northwestern University's Kellogg School of Management in 2008. After the acquisition of the social media listening company by a large research company, Scot moved onto his current path of leading marketing analytics teams in marketing agency leadership.

Scot joined Northwestern University's Master's Degree program in Integrated Marketing Communications as an Adjunct Lecturer from 2013 to 2017, where he taught "Statistics for Market Research" and developed and taught the program's first course on Marketing Science and Digital Analytics. The first edition of *Architecting Experience* was published in 2016.

Since then, Scot has continued to lead marketing analytics teams in the development and delivery of consumer intelligence and segmentation, targeting, propensity scoring, predictive modeling and response forecasting, budget allocation and channel planning, cross-channel performance evaluation, environmental trend analysis, testing, targeting and optimization. Over his career, Scot's clients have included Electronic Arts, AT&T, MasterCard, GSK, State Farm, USAA, Progressive, Humana, HP, GE, Yahoo!, Conagra, Diageo, Peapod and McDonald's.

In addition to marketing agency leadership, Scot manages Intelitecht Solutions, which advises and supports data/analytics-related start-ups and non-profits seeking to apply data-driven targeting and communications. Scot has turned his interest in education toward the development and delivery of online courses in media, culture, psychology and civics at the Center for Narrative Awareness.

Introduction

This second edition of *Architecting Experience* offers insights into the practice of conversion science; the methodological application of strategy, measurement, and analysis to the development and delivery of content, interfaces, and experiences to maximize the opportunity for transactions with consumers.

Whether working as a marketer using content as a means to motivate purchase, a maker using interfaces and experiences as the conduit to connect directly with consumers, or a publisher seeking to sell content as an end product, success requires approaching these efforts with meaningful data and analytics, clearly developed consumer insights, and sound consumer engagement strategies.

This second edition retains the aim of the first edition in answering what remains the most fundamental question facing anyone using media to fulfill their business objectives: "how do I motivate people to consume what I am offering?" And as it was in the first edition, the best answer to this remains: "through relevant and contextually delivered interfaces, content and experiences developed with insights from data and analytics".

The technologies and methodologies that are applied in achieving the answer above have changed enough in the years since the first edition to warrant a full refresh in this second edition's overview of digital data sources, communication technologies, and analytic methods — including digital assistants and voice search, geo-spatial data collection, and Augmented reality/Virtual reality (AR/VR) interfaces.

What has also changed since the first edition — and will only continue to develop after this edition is published — is the evolving "peer-to-peer" economics of making, selling, and communicating. The "long-tail" of goods, services, and content that emerged with the advent of digital communication has proliferated so that today there are often more alternatives to mainstream options than there are mainstream options. This means that entrepreneurs in almost any category can introduce their offerings to a large digital market. Each year a new crop of YouTubers grow themselves into full-fledged entertainment companies with large revenue streams coming from merchandising and advertising. Publishers of content, sellers of services, renters of vacation properties, and makers of everything from home furnishings to food products to arts, crafts, and games (to name a few) can sell direct to consumer (D2C) through their own channels or through platforms like Airbnb, Etsy, and Amazon. Digitized operations and logistics platforms enable professional-level distribution operations and support to the smallest business. And of course, digitized content distribution platforms make access to all kinds of advertising outlets, from addressable TV and online video to social media to ad targeting to email marketing, available to any business with budget to market themselves.

But perhaps the most significant change in this edition is the evolution from a focus specifically on problems of practice in marketing and media to what this edition newly defines as a discipline of "Conversion Science". The first edition's structure was built around digital marketing communications, and the ways in which roles and budgets have traditionally been assigned in large organizations — with specializations around "channels" of marketing that separate the teams working on "social" from those on "digital" from those working on "media" and so on. This structure was meant to help readers pinpoint the measurement and analytics skills they needed for their sphere of responsibility within a marketing communications practice.

The first edition of *Architecting Experience* included the definition of how analytics-driven practice in strategy, planning, content publishing, and experience design should be built on a full picture of consumers and their engagement with brands through multiple stages of their decision-making process and in every channel where they can be reached. This edition recognizes that this is not a set of interests limited only to marketing; they are applicable to anyone engaging consumers with content.

In fact, marketing is changing right along with changes in media and communications approaches in general, and all practices that are built around content are increasingly blurring together. Marketing for example is continuing to evolve from the mass-message based advertising that was once its central activity into broader multi-channel and multi-touch content and experience design in its ongoing effort to build a consistent connection between sellers and consumers. Increasingly, sellers are developing "content studio" capabilities to develop their own content in support of their offerings. And of course, news and entertainment businesses continue to need more content for more people spending more time on more screens with more and more diverse and disparate interests.

The changing ways that those with an interest in architecting experiences must think of consumers today is another dynamic reflected in this edition. European and US privacy laws have come into enforcement since the first edition was published. Social platforms have limited the availability of data accessible to third parties through permissions and APIs. These changes are welcome in the eyes of this author, as they reduce the possibility that content targeting and digital experiences are built on unwanted *surveillance*, and will instead increasingly challenge the conversion scientist to explicitly solicit information that consumers would then willfully offer around their wants and needs. In short, a turn from surveilling and manipulating to listening and responding.

Additionally, this edition encourages all of us who use data to create and target content with the intent of shaping consumers' behavior to consider the consequences of those behaviors. The modern blue-print for the use of content design and targeting to manipulate consumers' perspective and behaviors is well established through the US Senate's 2019 report on the Russian Internet Research Agency. "By flooding social media with false reports, conspiracy theories, and trolls, and by exploiting existing divisions, Russia is trying to breed distrust of our democratic institutions and our fellow Americans" wrote one Senator. Yes, reinforcing people's preconceptions and fueling their fears and prejudices can lead to desired outcomes when those outcomes are discord and chaos. It is anticipated that those are not the desired outcomes that most of this book's readers are seeking — so the tactics related to manipulation of harmful emotions should not be used as a template. Nor should the idea of manipulation in general.

By definition, consumers are individuals with an objective to acquire and consume an offering to fulfill a need or want. Content producers of every variety — from advertisers to publishers — should take responsibility for recognizing whether the fulfillment of the want or need is good for individuals independently and as a society. A lack of regulation against something that has potential or clear negative results does not make it right, and those of us working with data to convince consumers to consume should think about the rights and wrongs of consumption of specific types of offerings, but also of consumption in general. Consumption carries cost for the consumer, so we should have an ethical concern for the micro-economic impact of the conversions we are driving. Consumption (and the production that precedes it) uses natural resources and can create waste — so we should have an ethical concern for the environmental impact of the conversions we are driving. Physical consumption impacts the body — so we should have an ethical concern for the health impact of the conversions we are driving.

Those of us working with data to drive consumption must be more than objectively neutral observers who simply point others to where the data says the most of a desired outcome can be generated. Evaluation is an aspect of analysis: and if we hope to keep the consumer economy on a sustainable and collectively beneficial course, then we should accompany those insights with evaluation of the desired outcomes themselves and the consequences of fulfilling them.

With those broader concerns in mind, let's turn to how this book will take a more detailed dive into the aims and ideas discussed in this introduction.

The first five chapters of this book will provide you with the theoretical foundations of how content works to drive consumer behavior, as well as some practical guidance on how to plan and organize efforts around these foundations.

Chapters 6–8 will provide a survey of over 20 methods for engaging consumers, from television to digital assistants and e-commerce, and practical guidance on how to plan and optimize consumer experience through these channels.

The ninth chapter focuses on the possible uses of data, including concerns for privacy, and the methods by which advanced data science is applied to conversion optimization. Chapter 10 focuses on some social science considerations around data-driven conversion optimization.

On completion of this book, you will have gained actionable insights built on a solid foundation in marketing and consumer behavior theory, an understanding of marketing methods with a conversion focus, and insights into the technical, cultural, and organizational concerns that can drive or hinder advancement of data-driven consumer experience.

If this sounds useful to you, then let's get started.

Chapter ONE
Content Creates Consumer Experience

There was a time not even a century ago when it took relatively few words and images to move the world. In the 1930s and 1940s, impassioned and often poisoned words carried across radio waves, newspaper pages, and cinema newsreels to stir whole nations into action for good and for evil. Through the following decades, words and images in print, over radio, through film, and on television had the power to force moral examinations and accelerate social change; examinations leading to the erosion of the type of power that would use police dogs and fire hoses against protests for civil rights, or national guards with live ammunition to counter protests against a draft-fueled war, or napalm on civilians in the same war that was sending teenagers home to the US in body-bags by the day. Facts committed to newspaper pages were believed to be facts, and as such had the power to trigger a chain of events that would end in the resignation of a US President. And images provided inspiration as well, with families huddled around televisions to see rockets carrying the first humans ever to walk on the moon, or students standing up to the tanks of their totalitarian leaders, or the citizens of a city taking hammers to a wall that marked not just the end of the division of their city, but of the cold war as well.

This media that moved the world did so because its reach was concentrated on masses of people. Before the expansion of television from a few broadcast channels into hundreds of cable networks and the advent of digital communications, there were far fewer channels for content distribution, and significant economic capital was required in order to access them. Content made for mass distribution had no real competition beyond a few choices; mass media was what was there to pay attention to. So the narratives that passed through these mass media tended to generate mass impact, whether that be the bearing of witness to (and inspiration to participate in) cultural and social movements, or just a prosaic inspiration to consume what was being advertised in order to have the promised better life, or at least keep up with the Joneses.

Today, all of those spoken and written words of the past and the new ones of the present, the images still and moving that defined their times and now live as history, and that define our time as it happens; they are just a few million of the infinite molecules that make up the sea of content in which we all swim each day. Contemporary words that are meant to provoke or inspire, stories of corruption and cruelty at local, national, and international scales, images of miracles and disasters, of subjugation and resistance — all competing with selfies and food shots, with agenda-chasing political tweets, with professional YouTubers and embarrassing candid videos, with an increasing array of targeted advertising and content in on-demand services; an endless and unrelenting stream of content which no one can fully absorb. There is so much content competing for attention that it seems near impossible for anything to demand attention. And it is no longer just economic capital that drives what gets content noticed, it is also the more ephemeral and democratic currency of cultural capital. And the assignment of value to partisan narratives of the world leads some media consumers to uncritically accept certain sources of content as truth and reject other sources as lies, without any actual validation of how well what they accept as truth aligns with verifiable facts.

This is the state of our media environment today — all content is just more content — and whatever manages to get attention is good content on that basis, regardless of its composition. So more and more content is churned out — because there's money to be made and fame to be had and advantage to be gained when content captures attention. A video going viral turns an obscure comedian into a spokesperson for a global brand. YouTubers who have been posting into the void suddenly earn enough subscribers from stunts to develop themselves into the millionaire owners of media companies. Conspiracists and trolls get the satisfaction of seeing and hearing absurd ideas that should have stayed deep in underground news groups instead of being spread through "mainstream" media until they are referenced by talking heads on 24-hour news. Professional agitators with political agendas manipulate fears and prejudices to create chaos that softens societal underpinnings enough to make a bit more room for their agendas. Content publishers in news and entertainment continue to do their jobs by seeking to maximize profits from what they publish (and publish what creates the most profit).

Anyone hoping to convey a legitimate message that will drive the behavior of others has all of this to contend with. And when the stakes are high — as in a global viral pandemic — it is painfully clear how difficult it can be to convert people's entrenched beliefs and behaviors into action around a central set of facts. Communicators will have all kinds of behavioral objectives in mind. In a pandemic, it is to instill a sense of collective responsibility for care of self and others. For economic growth, it is conversion to a subscription or sale which is the primary focus in these pages. The communicators who are able to apply content to drive behaviors in other people — whether as crisis management, advocacy, agitation, art, or advertising — have likely set out with a clear goal, clear targets in who they are trying to influence, and an understanding of how content can be designed for and delivered to those targets to make it more than a drop in the ocean, even if just for a moment.

1.1 Experiencing Content

Content is everywhere in the form of media and in physical experience. It is like air — in endless supply, and consumed just as regularly. Books provide an ancient yet still effective portal to worlds within pages. Mobile devices put essentially infinite streams of content into our hands to be drawn into our experience of any moment. Headphones, speakers, and screens provide soundtracks and visuals that dominate or accent our movement through the day. On the street, content from shop signs to billboards reach out their visual tendrils to try and draw our attention as we move through the world.

What makes content meaningful to any given individual is its fit with their experience at the moment of contact. What makes content fit is its ability to garner attention while serving — versus interrupting — the consumer's intent in that moment.

Like any commodity, content is delivered through a supply chain in the hope of fit to a moment and attention capture. In this supply chain, suppliers have derived some source of content and refined it for their intended market, though the sources and refinement can range from selfie videos of silly dances to professionally written, produced, and edited assets. The supplier also has access to infrastructure and methods for distributing the refined product into the market.

Digital and social media advances have drastically expanded the terrain in which content sources can be discovered. Justin Bieber's career is an extreme but not isolated case; an amateur YouTube posting in 2008 leading to fame and fortune by 2010. Whatever a person's art, ability, or skill — digital distribution has made it possible to gain exposure and scale in ways that circumvent the "it's who you know" world of agents, producers, and distributors that was required to enter publishing and entertainment as recently as the first decade of the 21st century. As with Bieber, the major media companies are still converting talent to profits as they always have — and remain the gold-standard of success for many content makers — but they're no longer the primary source of content that streams into each of our lives.

The ubiquity and simplicity of digital publishing allows anything that anyone desires to be shared to have a chance at reaching an audience. But the most highly refined sources of content reach audiences through the established distribution methods of professional content publishers, which still include the publishing houses, studios, and media conglomerates of the late 20th century, along with new entrants in digital distribution like Spotify for music and Hulu for television, Netflix for video of all sorts, and Amazon for everything.

The value that premium content has for its audiences is expressed in the ability of these distributors (who are also increasingly becoming producers, and vice versa) to extract direct payment for their content anywhere from movie theater ticket windows to monthly content subscriptions. The "experience" of finding, accessing, and consuming content is an area of differentiation for competitors in this space. The type of content available is an important factor in the user experience (UX), but so is the ease of the user interface (UI) that allows a consumer to find and view what they want when and where they want it, as well as the interactions they have with the offering around billing, support, and the ability to upgrade or downgrade their service. It is not just the content, but also the experience built around the content that allows content publishers to make money directly from content delivery.

For subscription-based offerings, an advertising-free option is often a very important aspect of the premium UX. Content publishers can extract extra dollars from consumers in exchange for freedom from advertising as they consume content.

The more plentiful sources of less refined content reach audiences for free through social media channels and ad supported digital. Here is where what should be common knowledge holds true: "if the product is free, then YOU are the product".

User-generated content is delivered in digital placements and social-media streams through data-driven algorithms that have been designed and are continually refined to most effectively match content with people who will respond to it. The repeated response of people to types of content converts them into the base for advertisers' "audiences": groups of consumers organized by data about who they are and how they spend their time and money.

Though millions of consumers subscribe to ad-free content of all kinds, the majority of content available still remains ad-supported. Even after paying for a ticket to a movie or an airplane trip, the content you see is wrapped in advertising. Consumers of content are inevitably members of target audiences for advertisers. Knowing that the definition of "premium" subscription content delivery involves the exclusion of advertising — advertisers understand that to be effective, their content must try to align with, or at least not disrupt, the information or entertainment objectives consumers have in accessing the content where their ads are being placed. Going forward, if advertising is going to be part of the content consumption experience, it must try to complement the experience.

Experiencing Advertising

The first step in delivering an effective advertising experience is reaching the right audiences in a format that doesn't repulse them. But this is only a first step. Delivery of content that an audience will consume is the end objective of publishers.

Advertisers must reach a next step of shaping purchase behavior through that content.

Most advertisers understand that it takes more than one successful delivery of an ad to a consumer to impact that consumer's perception of the brand or decision to purchase. So advertising must take a longer view of the consumer's journey from awareness of their product to a decision to purchase, and maintain an "experience" of the brand through content-based advertising along the way.

The belief that advertising's effectiveness increases with multiple deliveries of relevant content is an evolution that has developed with the breadth of content available to consumers. In early advertising, placements were limited by the nature of media formats, appearing in print publications and out of home (OOH) options like posters and billboards. Because channel selection was simple, advertising energy and investment was put into creative design.

Over time, as media formats for content publishing expanded into television and later into digital, the options in media exposures expanded as well. As each of these expansions of access to consumers took place, the practices around buying media evolved to evaluate who was being accessed through any media purchase and the expected value of a media buy based on how those consumers were expected to behave. What media agencies offer today is the specialized ability to buy media at scale for targeted audiences, using data to select the most effective channels across the widest possible array of publishers, broadcasters, and other media channels.

With the continuing development of data-driven specialization within media strategy, and the consolidation of buying into large holding company agencies that have scale on their side, advertising services have split into media agencies who focus on acquiring audiences, and creative agencies who create the messaging that reaches those audiences. And the proliferation of media channels and formats with the emergence of digital has caused additional splits, with new forms of specialized agencies emerging around digital advertising, and even further specialization into social media marketing, influencer marketing, search engine marketing, and direct digital marketing to name a few.

The branching of marketing communications work into specializations that separate creative development from audience targeting and further fragment these by type of publishing tactic has resulted in an approach to marketing communications delivery that has become quite complex.

As today's marketers attempt to get consumers to think about them in their shopping moments, they must anticipate multiple possible paths a consumer can take for encounters with advertising on the way to their moment of purchase. And the media environment where consumers can be found has diffused from only a few channels owned by professional media companies to thousands of content publishers reaching audiences across traditional and digital formats, and millions of pieces of user-generated content flowing through social media users' streams.

Furthermore, marketers are not just trying to get customers to the store anymore. Working backwards from a sales objective, consumers' paths to purchase can terminate in any number of retail scenarios; in physical stores, in e-commerce retail like Amazon or Walmart.com, or for many brands, in direct online sale to consumers (D2C). Each brand's understanding of where they are being purchased now, who is buying and who isn't, and how they might shift points of purchase over time to increase sales to various consumer segments are critical aspects of not just their marketing strategy, but their overall business strategy.

Working across Figure 1.1, from each consumer and their motivation (on the left) to purchase (on the right), the first thing we develop after understanding our consumers is the "creative design" of content to be published in traditional and digital formats. Proceeding from this creative platform (hopefully **Figure 1.1** built against segments and motivations), we then Planning to develop content to reach consumers through adver- Purchase tising, direct marketing, CRM and email marketing, Flowchart and search. Despite all targeting the same consumer,

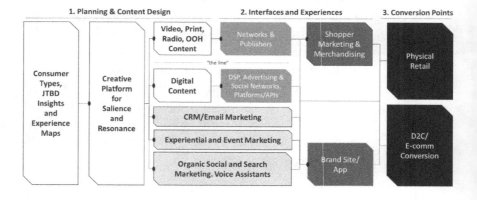

these efforts are still often planned and managed separately inside an advertiser's organization as they are managed by different internal teams, funded by different budgets, and even supported by separate specialized marketing agencies.

Distributing a variety of content to engage and persuade consumers falls in many cases to engagement with media agencies, and inevitably to interfaces with "marketing technology" and purchasing/publishing technologies for social media, search, and email, which may be handled internally or by agencies. The objective of these content distribution partners and tools is to put this content in front of targeted consumers through media that can include professionally-managed digital and traditional format publishers and broadcasters (including "native" editorial advertising, digital radio, and "connected television" like Hulu and other streaming services), social media platforms (i.e. Facebook, Instagram, and YouTube) with their "user-based" publishers and social influencers, search engines (and their voice-enabled assistant expansions into phones and homes), and potentially even the brand's website. Digital marketing can lead to "click-through" for sales through a direct to consumer sales platform, or to a third-party online retail platform like Amazon. com where a sale can take place.

Advertising in non-digital publications, OOH, and much of digital media however is not able or expected to drive click-through to sale, but remains a part of putting the brand in front of audiences. Direct mail, email, print, television and radio ads, digital "impressions" without clicks, website visits, social content views are all hoped to assist a conversion at a later point; in eventual online shopping or in a visit to a bricks and mortar store. To assist in that happening, marketing may retarget certain consumer behaviors with subsequent ads, or may reach out to lists they've collected. To follow up on the brand awareness it is hoped is developed by their ad "impressions", marketing also employs "lower funnel" tactics that help reach shoppers when they're shopping with various in-retail display tactics, and that work with sellers to most effectively price and present the brands' merchandise in ways that increase placement in consumers' baskets.

Experiencing "Media"

The advertising approaches above would not be possible without a "media" ecosystem to enable their delivery. Given the breadth and depth of any individual's exposure to media today, it seems inconceivable that the phrase "media" and the concepts associated with it would at one time have required an introduction to popular thinking, but in fact there was such a time not that long ago, and the man who made the introduction was Professor Marshall McLuhan.

McLuhan's 1965 book *Understanding Media: The Extensions of Man* introduced the concept of "media" where previously there had simply been notions of independent communication technologies such as "the press", "radio", and "television" which were recognized to synthesize into a single unit in practice, but were nonetheless typically evaluated individually with regards to their impact on culture.

McLuhan observed that these and many other information and communication technologies and practices not only work together and proceed from one another, but that in doing so they actually extend the perceptual power of individuals and mediate communication and thinking in ways that significantly influence culture and human affairs; thus his application of the term "media" to these mediating "extensions of man".

Perhaps the most lasting convention introduced by McLuhan (and the most useful for the subject of this book) is the notion of "hot" and "cool" media, or elements of culture. Very few people wonder who should be credited for coining the use of "cool" in social context, e.g. a "cool" new band or the "cool" kids at school, since the expression seems to have always been a part of the vernacular. Equally, the idea of a "hot" new sound or a person with a "hot" body are commonly used in American parlance without consideration of origin. Today, these notions of "cool" and "hot" seem natural in the ways they are applied, but it was just as recently as the beginning of the Cold War that Marshall McLuhan observed that different media exerted different influences on people's perceptions and engagement with those media, and classified those media into "hot" and "cold" categories.

McLuhan's theory has held up well into the early 21st century media environment, and still provides an excellent framework for understanding the influence of mediated information on culture, and the countervailing response of culture in the subsequent development of new information technology. Everyone wants their content to be "hot", "sticky", and "viral", and these metaphors for information owe much to McLuhan's understanding of how people engage with messages in media. To boil down the application of McLuhan's ideas on marketing to a fundamental principle — a message is either relevant in a receiver's current context, or it is not.

As any frustrated screenplay author or aspiring comedian or YouTube video maker or freelance writer knows, this is the rule for content creators and publishers. It is not enough to have content developed; the content maker must also understand how to get what they have to say or show in front of people who will care, and in a way that will pull attention from everything else that consumer could have looked at to see their work instead. Then, they must convert that attention into a level of engagement with their content. And to have engagement with their content repeated by the same consumers over time, they must create a positive sense of experience around that engagement.

Because social networks leave the production of content to their users — their popularity is built on the experience they provide in delivering content for consumption. Content makers welcome the tools that increase their opportunity to be discovered through content promotion algorithms. And content consumers love having a stream that is "personalized" to align with the type of content they've consumed in the past.

The UX in content consumption matters everywhere. A large differentiation between streaming video options and the cable format they are replacing comes from a UX that delivers simplicity of set-up and provides easy support if there's any confusion, and from UIs that drive algorithmic recommendations and simplify the organization and consumption of content anywhere, at any time.

YouTube channels raise millions of followers by encouraging a shared experience; asking viewers to like and subscribe in response to the actions of characters in the video.

Success in publishing and distribution requires that the experience consumers have with content is close to seamless, with content that is well aligned with the consumer's interest. When access to the content is free, consumers may accept a few misses in the relevance of content being offered to them, just as they will accept some advertising content as a part of their stream. However, even that advertising will need to have some entertainment value and other relevance, or there's a chance consumers will be repulsed by advertising that isn't as targeted to their interests as the content they came for — harming both the advertiser and the publisher. And when publishers use free content as "bait" to try and draw users into a subscription, unless the content has no reasonable substitute, the infinite sea of content consumers can return to as an alternative may make the paywall too high a hurdle for consumers to care to cross.

Premium offerings requiring payment for their consumption will be held to very high standards of UX in terms of the offering itself and the UI that facilitates its consumption. In fact, the UX requirements around direct payment for content are similar to those required in putting any offering online for purchase directly by the consumer. Whether an offering available for sale is a mattress or clothing or food or news or entertainment:

1. it must gain the attention of consumers and build their intent to purchase,
2. it must facilitate evaluation and purchase processes for consumers in ways that stand out from its competitors, and
3. to maintain subscriptions or cultivate the potential for repeat purchase, it must continue to support consumers after their initial purchase.

The first of these is marketing and advertising. The remaining two are UX efforts. All three require an understanding of consumers and how they respond to content at all levels of engagement with an offering.

Interfaces, Content, and Experience

The path to the consumption of an offering requires exchange between the seller and the buyer. Within this book, the collection of possible formats through which such exchange can take place will often be mentioned as interfaces, content, and experience.

Interfaces

Interfaces are the structures within which exchange takes place. In physical environments, the interface around a transaction includes the location's layout, the presentation of merchandise within the layout, and the flow through the location to checkout.

In digital environments, the interface is the way people interact with that environment through a device. UI design and the field of human–computer interaction (HCI) are devoted to understanding how to optimize an interface toward the goals of both the user and the presenter of that interface. The goal of digital interfaces should be to deliver the comprehensive set of capabilities the user could be seeking in the simplest and most intuitive way possible.

Content

Content is what consumers engage with as they interface with sellers. In physical retail environments, content is the sign above the door, what fills the shelves and covers the walls. It is the merchandise itself, and the way in which that merchandise is presented. Beyond retail, content is sold through magazines, newspapers, television and movies, live sports, concerts, theater, and dance, to name a few options. And advertising content reaches consumers through many of these same media, as well as through billboards, transit, on-premise sampling, and other OOH advertising.

In digital environments, content can be the product, as it is with social-media streams, entertainment, and news providers. Or — for advertising — content can be static or interactive text or visuals, editorial, video or audio, presented through these same social media, news, and entertainment offerings as well as via search engines and voice assistant responses.

Experiences

Experiences are defined by the nature and quality of an individual's interactions with content through the available interfaces. In both advertising and direct content consumption, the interface itself and the content provided are both critical aspects of a consumer's experience. An experience will not be perceived well if the interface does not intuitively and engagingly provide the ability to effectively interact with the offering, or if the content does not meet or hold the interest or intent that motivated engagement with the interface.

One aspect of content that frequently shapes experience is the quality of interpersonal engagement between the seller and consumer, which, in addition to the quality of interface and content, is referred to as customer experience (CX). In physical conversion environments, a significant aspect of the experience is based upon the quality of interaction provided by service staff.

For content providers, interaction with staff can take place as early as efforts to directly contact consumers for subscription sales, and includes how consumers' attempts to reach a real person by phone or email or text to change or cancel a subscription are handled. YouTubers and other social media-based publishers are engaging in CX when they engage directly with subscribers through comments on their sites. Direct to consumer online sales must have well-trained consumer contact representatives to help ensure that every aspect of a purchase including potential returns are a positive experience for consumers.

1.2 Conversion Science

As consumers engage with digital advertising and owned digital interfaces, existing data about their membership in an "audience" is applied to shape the engagement, and new data is created and collected as a result of the engagement. For advertisers, content publishers, media agencies, creative agencies, and e-commerce sellers to be successful in their work, they must understand who their work is meant to impact, and specifically how that impact can be delivered in a way that maximizes the target objective.

For media publishers — in writing, video, or interactive for news, entertainment, or games — the ultimate objective is the collection and retention of audiences (as readers, or viewers or users). Whether they pay for content directly or support content through advertising — content is a publisher's product and marketing is required to obtain and retain audiences with this content.

For advertisers, the ultimate objective is the sale of what they are offering. Driving these sales is the sellers' objective in hiring media and creative agencies, and the objectives of agencies themselves are derivatives of that sales objective. Media agency objectives tend to focus on getting the brand's marketing in front of as many people as possible for the best possible rates to maximize the return on advertising spend, while creative agencies may be evaluated on how their content is reacted to in digital environments where feedback by way of content engagement and sharing is immediate, and/or whether their overall creative work is somehow correlated with sales over a longer period of time.

In each of these cases, there is a need to define how objectives will be measured, to apply any available data that increases the chances for success, and to collect additional data that informs performance measurement and increases the ability to optimize performance. For each of the objectives described above, organizations require people to conduct the collection, connection, and application of data in ways that guide the development and delivery of content to audiences through media in ways that best deliver on objectives.

The application of data and technology to drive outcomes through media requires several areas of analytic focus. First and foremost, there is no sense in developing a plan to engage consumers with content through media without an understanding of the market and competitive environment. So business and market analytics must create a data-driven understanding of "how much" opportunity exists in the market.

In addition to knowing how much opportunity is available, successful marketing also requires bringing forward an offering that consumers want or need, and letting them know it's there. To make this happen, customer insights and performance analytics must play an integrated role in digital marketing design and execution. In a market moved by the facilitation of relevant experiences, the organization with the best understanding of their customers, the drivers of demand for offerings, and the most effective way to gain attention on the path to purchase have a clear advantage over competitors.

A common misconception about marketing is that it somehow creates the wants or needs that motivate consumers. Marketing does not create consumer's wants or needs. The psychological, sociological, and physiological drivers behind consumers' wants and needs exist prior to and independent of marketing. Through research, data collection, and analytics, marketing does however focus on identifying and understanding the drivers of these wants and needs as the basis for everything from product innovation and design to the way the value of the product is communicated to consumers, and analytics are applied throughout to understand both "how" and "how much" marketing works.

Figure 1.2 shows the consumer's path from motivation to purchase, and the relationship of data science and analytics practices to this path.

Figure 1.2 | Conversion Science Ecosystem

At the top-center of Figure 1.2 we see that the consumer's path to purchase begins with their motivations within contexts. These motivations (needs, wants, interests) are felt by an individual; someone with attitudes, beliefs, family, friends, and

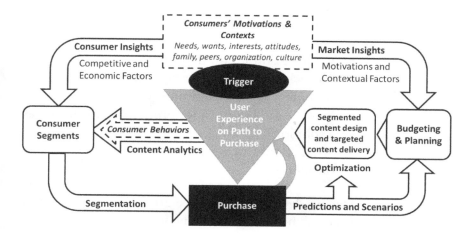

organizational ties. If this individual believes their motivation can be served through the consumption of an offering or offerings, it becomes the trigger — sending the user down the path to purchase.

"Consumer Insights" are drawn from the contexts of our consumer base, shown here extending from the left side of the motivations box. When filtered through the mesh of competitive and economic factors that shape consumption, consumer insights feed our ability to define distinctive consumer segments.

Also extending from consumer's motivations and contexts (on the top-right of Figure 1.2) we have "market insights", which inform us on the overall potential demand for our offering. When filtered through the mesh of motivations and contextual factors discovered through consumer insights, market insights inform our budgeting and planning for marketing communications. Some of the questions we will ask and answer here include:

- What are consumers seeking from the category currently?
- Which competitors are or aren't serving their needs?
- What substitutes do they have?
- For what gaps in nearby categories can we become a better substitute?
- By what methods can we promote our offering as a solution?
- What should we spend to have a positive return on spend for the sales we believe we can achieve?

Having determined who we are going to reach and what will be most compelling to them as a motivation to buy, and having assigned a budget for getting that in front of them, we then design content for each segment, and conduct targeting to reach those segments. This is delivered into the UX on their path to purchase. Response to this content is measured as an output of our process in two ways.

The most important measure of output resulting from this process of deploying content to the UX is the measure of purchases or sales. The entire basis for creating content to shape the UX on the path to purchase is that such effort produces incremental sales results.

Our other measure of output from the delivery of content into the UX is the measurement of consumer's behaviors as they move through their journey to purchase (or not). While we are looking at behaviors as the dependent variable, what we're analyzing here is the impact of content on those behaviors — so this is our area of content analytics.

Our analysis of how consumers respond to content in their experience with the brand on the path to sales should recognize the various segments we defined and used in the planning and development of that content. So, as shown in Figure 1.2, the measurement of consumer behaviors is organized by segments.

Those behaviors by segment are then mapped into our record of purchases to evaluate purchase by segment. This connection allows us to find correlation between the behaviors of different segments along the journey and the conversion rates of these segments at the end of the journey. These correlations then become the fuel for predictive models and scenarios that guide both the optimization of content in real-time to maximize conversions, and the budgeting and planning for subsequent content development for various segments.

Finally, at the bottom of Figure 1.2 there is a feedback loop from purchase directly into the UX on the path to purchase. This is expressing the influence that purchase and post-purchase consumption has on subsequent decisions to purchase or not. A positive process of purchasing and using the offering can prove that the marketing of the product was on-point and validate the consumer's decision to buy. A negative experience in purchasing or using the offering will create mistrust in prior and subsequent marketing. A good product experience is the best marketing possible for repeat conversions.

This exploration of Figure 1.2 has taken us quickly through all of the components of conversion science that will be developed in much greater detail throughout the rest of this book. To begin our in-depth analysis of driving conversion through content and experience, the next chapter unpacks how and why content can become effective in driving consumers to conversion.

Chapter TWO | Media Moves Markets

Books like this one exist because in a culture that is highly saturated with content seeking consumers' attention, it is difficult to deliver attention-earning and behavior-guiding content that guides the consumers' conversion to a desired result.

2.1 Media Product Conversion

For many content businesses, conversions are subscriptions. Traditional media like newspapers and magazines were originally built on subscription sales, with advertising revenue in only a secondary role. Broadcast television was entirely ad supported, then cable added subscriptions to the medium, which remains in place with streaming services. Social media is a free service to users supported entirely by advertisers.

When publishers deliver content (or a social media network provides a distribution channel for user generated content, or a gaming company releases a mobile game), they are striving to build or maintain an audience that they can monetize, either through direct subscription to or purchase of the content, or through free access to content (readership/viewership/play) in place of subscription to attract advertisers' purchase of access to their audience.

2.2 Business to Consumer Conversion

For business to consumer (B2C) retailers and the wholesale organizations that supply them, conversions are sales. Retailers track conversion of consumers' "baskets" — the collection of goods they take out of the store. And not just physical stores anymore of course — online retail still gives users a "cart" to fill, and the conversion is what's purchased from the cart. Wholesalers get conversions when one or more of the products in the cart are theirs. Of course, because these are sold through retailers, they're dependent on retailers for their data.

When B2C retailers and wholesalers deliver content, it is typically in the form of advertising or direct marketing — distributed through a variety of media, or through direct access to consumer contact information such as email lists or home addresses.

2.3 Business to Business Conversion

For business to business (B2B) sellers, conversion is a purchase of their offering by another business. B2B sales often occur through a contract and cover sales that are high volume, high cost or both. Because B2B sales are often high commitment in one of these ways, the path to purchase involves a great deal of research and comparison.

For this reason, when B2B sellers deliver content, it is often oriented toward education of a consumer, in a format that supports education. B2B seller's content is often more academic or journalistic in nature — providing real insight into changes and advances in the buyer's field of work, and offering education on approaches to navigating those changes and advances. Such educational professional content can deliver real benefit to readers/viewers/ listeners of industry newsletters, blogs, magazines, videos, and podcasts, but it comes at an expense to the producer, which they hope to offset in sales. However, the content is held to a journalistic standard, its value or interest in content can erode if the content seems too clearly un-objective and self-promotional — creating a compelling challenge in how to produce it well.

2.4 Creating Attention and Action

What is common across all of the conversion cases above is that each of them seeks to attract consumers with content that demonstrates the value of an offering, then generates a desired transaction from the consumer in response to that offering. For content publishers on topics ranging from news to entertainment, for retail and wholesale sellers, for services and in fact just for anyone selling B2B or B2C, that desired transaction is a sale. For publishers, it is the sale (or renewal) of a subscription to their content, or the purchase of a license. For everyone else, it is the purchase of whatever they have placed on the market. But for all of these businesses, content of some sort — a sample of entertainment or editorial or advertising about the offering — is first put in front of consumers for their free consumption to try and convert them to paid consumption of the offering behind it. And that, put simply, is marketing.

Somewhat more comprehensively, marketing is the practice of placing a good or service into a market, and connecting it with buyers. Successful marketing requires the visible placement of a product that consumers want to buy. The product will be successfully marketed if it is readily available to consumers when they are in the market, if its qualities and attributes meet consumers' requirements, if consumers know to look for it, and if the price is right for what is offered. It is expected that such successful marketing will lead to sales.

Challenges in this straightforward undertaking arise in two primary ways. The first is when a market comes to feature several competing products with very similar qualities and attributes; a category of products. In these cases, marketers seek to develop and emphasize qualities and attributes that raise their own visibility in the category and positively differentiate their product from others in the category. The principle of "branding" emerges here as an effort to create mental associations around a product that have little to do with the product's intrinsic attributes, but that instead inject extrinsic value into the product. In competitive markets for established products, the objectives of marketing (and the sales marketing promotes) are based on earning an increasing share of total purchase in the product category.

The second challenge in marketing arises when a new product is brought to market. In this case, consumers need to learn about the product's qualities and attributes, and determine the value they place on consuming these. For the first product to market, marketing's work is to help consumers immediately see the maximum value possible for the product, and to prepare to maintain an advantage through differentiation as imitators follow into the market. For the "fast-followers" into market, marketing's objective is to learn what consumers value in the new product and emphasize that in their product.

Laws of Growth

What is common across the challenges above is the core mission of marketing; make as many people as possible aware of why they should select your offering, and make it available for them to select.

In 2010, Professor Byron Sharp of the University of South Australia's Ehrenberg-Bass Institute for Marketing Science introduced several core concepts around how to achieve this core mission in his book "How Brands Grow: What Marketers Don't Know".

The core theme of his book is the idea that marketing effectiveness is subject to a set of "laws" which can be observed through a scientific method of experimentation and measurement. Like all laws, Sharp's "Laws of Growth" exert their influence within an environment that consequently allows observation of their effects. Sharp in fact observes two environments in which the laws of marketing are made effective.

The first is the sphere of consumers' "mental availability" around the brand. The mental availability of a brand is simply the degree to which a consumer will think about or notice a specific brand at the point of purchase. As Sharp explained in a 2011 blog post, "[t]he easier the brand is to access in memory, in more buying situations, for more consumers, then the higher the overall mental availability".

The second sphere in which marketing's laws have effect is around the offering's "physical availability". Creating mental availability for a brand in buying situations is only effective if the brand is also physically available in those same buying situations.

In essence, the propensity for any offering's sales exists at the intersection of this simple Venn diagram (Figure 2.1).

Thus, for marketers to drive growth, they must assess the current state of performance in delivering mental and physical availability for the brand within the context of its category and its complements or alternatives, and they must provide actionable insights to better establish and join these among the widest set

Figure 2.1
Creating Sales

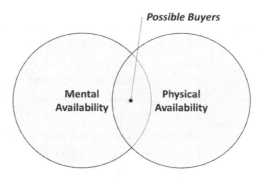

of consumers possible. Ideally, there should be mental availability among everyone for whom the offering has some fit, and there should be physical availability for everyone with mental availability.

Professor Sharp and his colleagues at the Ehrenberg-Bass Institute present several "Laws of Growth" in their book and in other writing. The primary "law" that most determines the overall effectiveness of marketing in the context of mental and physical availability is the law of "double jeopardy".

The law of double jeopardy is based on a pattern that was described by Sharp's colleague Andrew Ehrenberg in the 1970s. Ehrenberg's research showed that brands with smaller market share have two forces working against them. The first and most obvious jeopardy for smaller share brands is the fact that they have fewer customers than larger brands. The second jeopardy is that smaller brands' customers are less loyal to these smaller brands than they are to larger brands.

In understanding double jeopardy, it is important to recognize that in measurable terms, loyalty is based on metrics like number of purchases per customer and average defection, as well as attitudinal feedback like self-reported brand affinity. Lower loyalty in a category means fewer purchases per customer than higher loyalty brands, with lower affinity for the brand and a higher probability to stop buying from the brand.

The behavioral driver behind the double jeopardy law is the fact that consumers tend to shop within categories of goods and are very willing to switch across brands in a category for a number of reasons. Physical availability is one driver of those reasons, and larger brands have the resources to maintain more physical availability, and to more frequently lower the barriers to purchase with price-based merchandising tactics. Mental availability is another driver of selection across brands in a category, and larger brands have the resources to establish more effective memory patterns around their brands with more people, and with greater frequency in refreshing and reinforcing those patterns.

The consequence of these observations about how mental and physical availability drive growth under double-jeopardy is very straightforward and common-sensical, which makes it helpful to know that it is also supported in such substantial fact by researchers like Ehrenberg and Sharp.

In order to grow, a brand must increase its penetration of the category to reach buyers who currently do not buy their brand, or who buy it less frequently than other brands in the category. Thus, a first strategic and tactical challenge for marketing in driving growth is how to reach as many consumers as possible.

A second challenge is to ensure that as we reach as many consumers as possible, we are reaching them with messages that will most effectively establish and maintain positive mental availability for our brand.

Attention Economy

Successfully conveying the distinctive value of an offering to drive consumer behavior requires first capturing the attention of consumers so that they see and register a message that establishes mental availability. The ability for advertising to capture attention is an increasing challenge in our world of ever-present content competing for attention at every moment a consumer is engaged with media.

To gain attention and convert that attention into a unit of mental availability for an offering, marketers must understand the mechanics of what earns people's attention, and how it happens.

The process of decision making has been most clearly described by Daniel Kahneman, who won a Nobel Prize in Economic Sciences in 2002 for his work on the topic, and who translated that work for popular understanding in his 2011 book *Thinking Fast and Slow*.

As described in the book's title, Kahneman's work (which has been independently validated many times over) has established that our mental processing operates under two systems. "System 1" is our always-on processing system, which is built for automatic snap-responses to what life sends our way. This is the "thinking fast" aspect of our mental processing which developed as a core function for our survival to escape from danger, but which has evolved to include anything we can do as "second nature", including what we consider highly expert in-the-moment "choices" made by experienced athletes, surgeons, pilots, managers, and so on. Kahneman also labels this system as our *autopilot*.

Kahneman's "System 2" is our slow system. This is the deliberate process of reflection and consideration that we recognize as thinking. Mental processing under System 2 involves much more effort than System 1's reflexive responses. This is the mental process that results in the observation that someone is "deep in thought", or even "lost in thought". This is the approach to thinking that applies logic, that utilizes critical approaches and that evolves on abstract lines of association.

Advertising is targeted at encoding and triggering System 1 mental processing, and the application of Decision Science principles can allow advertising and marketing to leverage the "System 1" framework to build mental availability that may influence choice at the time of purchase.

However eventually consumers will evaluate their decision in the slower more rational "System 2" frame. Marketers must understand that if the reality of a consumer's purchase does not match what they came to believe about the product through their "System 1" thinking process, they will feel regret over their decision. Not only will they then likely avoid the offering at the next point of purchase, but many of them will share their regret and disappointment in a way that creates negative attitudes within the mental availability around the brand.

Aligning System 1 perceptions with the reality encountered through System 2 is therefore a core requirement for sustaining successful marketing. For this to happen, marketers should seek to ensure that what gains consumers attention about their offering is actually and recognizably delivered in some way through their offering.

Jobs to Be Done

The wants and needs of consumers that drive their decision to buy are not always answered by what an offering provides directly through its attributes, features, and functionality. Be it apparel, accessories, footwear, makeup, mid-size sedans, cable packages, mobile carrier, checking accounts, fast-casual dining options, hotel rooms, condo units, ketchup bottles, cans of beans, bottled water brands, or most any other product in any other category; the real differences in features and functions between most offerings in most categories are not tangible enough to warrant a decision to buy one or another on the offering's attributes alone.

The mental availability we establish for our brand to support a decision at the point of purchase will be weak if it is based solely on establishing that our offering is available for purchase with a set of features and functions. Mental availability is strongest when consumers understand how the offering is able to achieve something that matters to them beyond the features and functions it delivers. For most consumers there is a very perceptible difference between a Rolex watch and a Timex watch despite their extreme similarity in the function of telling their wearer the time. Consumers who want a Rolex over a Timex do not simply want to spend more money for the same functionality they could get for less in another option. They believe they are buying something more than just the watch's ability to tell time, or even the quality of the materials, something that is worth more to them than just the product attributes alone.

Harvard Business School professor Clayton Christenson described the "something more" that consumers are seeking from goods and services as the product's "Job To Be Done (JTBD)". Understanding what drives a consumer's valuation of a product and willingness to buy requires understanding what job the consumer is "hiring" the product to do for them.

In a 2016 Harvard Business Review article, Christenson provided the story of a real estate developer who was having trouble selling new condominium units. They had been designed for people who were downsizing their housing, and the market at that moment for such people was strong, but the units weren't converting as planned. So the developer conducted research with the people who had already purchased units from him to understand the steps that led up to their decision.

A surprising insight emerged; people kept bringing up their dining room table, and the need to figure out what to do with it before they moved. The condo units being sold were designed to help people downsize, so they had not been designed to hold a dining room table. But the emotional attachment that prospective movers felt to their dining room table was something that hadn't been considered in the product design.

Christensen quotes the developer as telling him "I went in thinking we were in the business of new-home construction, but I realized we were in the business of moving lives". And with this realization, the developer had identified the JTBD by his entire offering. It wasn't just the layout and finishes of the units — though they did some redesign to make room for a kitchen table. The building also began offering a moving service, two years of storage, and a post-move sorting room in the building.

Emphasizing how their building fulfilled a JTBD helped the business. They were able to raise prices, and grew their business by 25% while the industry faced a 49% downturn.

The JTBD that consumers were "hiring" against when considering moving was not simply about finding a new place to live. This condo developer could not create a want or need to move — marketing for the building was not putting the idea of moving into people's heads. People who were considering moving had a reason for moving: to downsize and simplify. But many had a conflicting reason not to move: the emotional attachment to their old home, and the things in it.

All of these consumer attitudes toward the possibility of moving were shaped by factors other than marketing, and the marketing and sales process was required to work within them. And to work within them, the way the product was marketed couldn't just showcase attributes of the product, it needed to explain why the product should be "hired" to fulfill an important job for the consumer.

To successfully market an offering as a prospective hire for a JTBD, Christensen defines several requirements. Marketers must look beyond demographics and their offering's features and functions to understand the circumstances around the buying behavior. Within these circumstances, we must consider the social and emotional dimensions that create a challenge or point of stress that the offering can be hired to solve. And the offering's qualifications to solve the problem should be distinctive; addressing the problem in a way that is only partially addressed or unaddressed by other options.

The Consumer Experience and Consumer Journey

The circumstances a consumer encounters and their behaviors as they determine how to fulfill a need are commonly described as consumer experience and the consumer decision journey.

In 2009, McKinsey Consulting introduced the idea of the consumer decision journey to provide a more nuanced standard in thinking about the path consumers take from awareness through purchase and beyond than was provided by the common notion of a "purchase funnel".

The traditional notion of a consumer's path to purchase has been one of movement through a funnel (Figure 2.2). At the beginning of the process is a wide entrance, representing the breadth of reach

Figure 2.2
The Conversion
Funnel

and awareness that an offering tries to create with marketing to as large a consumer audience as possible. Then there are forces that drive that broad reach down into a much narrower flow of customers. And this was the problem with the funnel concept. It describes what happened in the market (only a small proportion of the total prospect base converts), but it does not explain how or why. It simply asserts that there are forces that make a broad base of reach turn into a more narrow flow of conversion.

McKinsey's consumer decision journey introduces a model that helps explain what might be happening in between the development of awareness and the decision to convert to an offering or not.

Figure 2.3 takes the original notions of the McKinsey customer decision journey and adds two additional dimensions: the role of external "life events" as "triggers" to the customer decision journey, and the interaction points between customers on the journey and data about those customers.

The process begins on the far left with a *life event*, which is some piece of context that provides the

Figure 2.3
The Customer
Decision
Journey

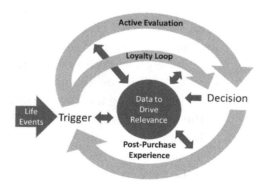

motivation to take action in our product category. Life events are diverse, and the life events that make an offering relevant to a consumer will vary based on the nature of that offering. Life events can range from major events such as marriage, a new job, a new house, or the birth of a child to everyday events such as hosting a party or even just having time for lunch, reaching the weekend, getting off from work in the afternoon, or needing toilet paper. Life events do not need to be major in order to be significant triggers for the customer decision process. The size and scope of the life event is not what matters. What matters most is that marketers are cognizant of the fact that there is always an external context to a customer's entry into a decision journey — that the customer has a life outside the decision process, and that something about that life brought them in to the decision process. Understanding this, the marketer should treat life events and the resulting motivations as something important enough to their customer to trigger the expenditure of thought and energy through the decision process, and should of course recognize that the more significant the life event, the more significant the customer problems, objectives, and needs.

From the triggering event and resulting motivation, we proceed clockwise through the diagram. Customers in the first round of the journey will travel around the outside path labeled "active evaluation". While on this path of active evaluation, they are developing an "initial consideration set" around the options available to them to address the problems, objectives, and needs established with the triggering event. This is where mental availability begins to be established.

To survive the active evaluation stage, brands must achieve attention for their offering, then begin banking mental availability for the consumer to reference at their decision point. To get consumers attention and build mental availability, understanding and referencing what is already meaningful to the consumer is the fastest path to relevance. This is the core principle behind behavioral and contextual targeting and content optimization.

Moving clockwise along the diagram, the customer moves through their active engagement and ultimately reaches a decision. If the trigger was not strong enough to overcome dissatisfaction with all of the options considered, then the customer may decide not to make a purchase at all. If the trigger was strong but no option was truly satisfactory, then the customer will likely select entirely on cost and convenience. And if during active consideration one option differentiated itself according to the customer's needs, at this point the decision will be made to purchase from that brand.

Continuing clockwise around the consumer decision journey, the next stage focuses on the post-purchase, or post-decision, experience that the customer has with a brand. Typically, this is thought of as "Customer Relationship Management" (CRM) and "customer service" for customers who have bought something from us.

This is often the only segment of the target population that a company will engage at this stage in the journey. But those customers whose decision led to the choice of an offering other than ours still can and should also be engaged here. For those potential customers who chose another option, our post purchase engagement will be focused largely around paid media. Having provided that level of relevance in their experience, we then use data to anticipate their future needs and to be ready to deliver greater relevance when they reach their next trigger.

For active customers, engagement in the post-decision stage of the journey is the key to guiding them into the "loyalty loop". This "loyalty loop" comes from establishing a strong preference for our brand with the customer so that at the next trigger, the customer's active evaluation will default to our company's options and will bypass the "active evaluation" of our competitors.

Conversion Analytics

As consumers move down a path to conversion on their journey, sellers' efforts to influence them are best served through the collection of data, and application of analysis.

Gaining consideration at the beginning of a path to conversion requires analysis that understands and addresses how to create mental availability for the brand within the context of its category and its complements or alternatives. This requires analysis of consumer attitudes and behaviors, and of the market and competitors.

Successfully conveying the distinctive value of an offering to drive consumer behavior requires first capturing the attention of consumers so that they see and register the message. And the ability for advertising to capture attention is an increasing challenge in our world of ever-present content competing for attention at every moment a consumer is engaged with media.

Advertising is targeted at triggering System 1 mental processing to build mental availability that may influence choice at the time of purchase. The mental availability we establish for our brand to build support for a decision at the point of purchase will be weak if it is based solely on establishing that our offering is available for purchase with a set of features and functions. Mental availability is strongest when consumers understand how the offering is able to achieve something that matters to them beyond the features and functions it delivers.

Thinking of the "JTBD" by our offering gives us that "something more". To convey value, we must understand that what drives a consumer's valuation of a product and their willingness to buy is the extent to which the consumer can "hire" the offering to do a job for them in a better way than other options.

Marketers must look beyond demographics and their offering's features and functions to understand the circumstances around the buying behavior. Within these circumstances, we must consider the social and emotional dimensions that create a challenge or point of stress that the offering can be hired to solve.

The circumstances that a consumer encounters and their behaviors as they work out how to fulfill a need are commonly described as consumer experience and the consumer decision journey. Both of these must be actively addressed through interfaces, content, and experience to motivate consumers to convert.

And it is the collection of data around engagement with User Interface (UI), content, and experience that teaches publishers and sellers how to optimize interfaces, content, and experiences to increase their influence within the consumer journey.

Chapter THREE

Data is the "New Oil": Analytics are Advanced Chemistry

3.1 The Challenge to "Collect and Connect"

The Latin root of the word "data" means "a given/a thing", and that's all data is; a collection of givens. Data is the source from which information can be created, but it is not quite information in itself. The transition of a set of givens from data to information requires analysis. Putting it in terms of a coin flip; data is the possession of a coin with one side up, analysis is the ability to contrast the sides of the coin, and information is the recognition of specifically which side is up.

So, in thinking of data, we are thinking of what "givens" we can collect with which to generate information, insights, and action. As analysts, every insight we generate and every action we recommend is grounded in our data, so every analyst must take accountability for their data as one of the most fundamental aspects of their work.

As discussed in the preceding section, the sources of data around consumer's interests and engagement with interfaces, content, and experience are all widely dispersed, and the first challenge of analysis for conversion science is to collect and connect these sources. There are three fundamental challenges in the collection and connection of digital marketing data:

1. the data is scattered across platforms and communication channels,
2. with access constrained by organizational silos,
3. and it is of questionable quality as its generation has largely been an afterthought.

The unfortunate state of analytics around consumers interactions with interfaces, content, and experiences today is that much of the available data is generated as exhaust without any pre-defined design for its structure and collection, and much of the data that would be of most value is not captured, as its collection has not been explicitly designed. And if the design and collection of data has not been as deeply strategized and designed as the creative and technology aspects, the availability of any data for useful analysis will be a lucky accident.

The Disjointed Nature of Data

The process of overcoming data collection challenges and building an accurate and comprehensive data repository for digital marketing analytics begins with an understanding of the types of data and the ways in which data can be generated and applied.

A well-known description of big data is built around the factors of variety, velocity, and volume, with "big data" being big because it possesses one or more of these qualities; it comes from many sources, it comes quickly, and/or it comes in large volumes.

Variety

Historically, the most common data used in the design of interfaces, content, and experience comes from smaller scale qualitative research that measures behavioral and attitudinal response through panels, ethnographic observation, and usability labs.

These methods collect data from samples of a population at a fixed point in time. The insights from a sample at a fixed point in time are then extrapolated onto the population and considered applicable to the present moment. While this method can generate very good "directional" insights, as a sample taken at a point in time from a fixed position, it is much like recording a concert performance on a smartphone camera, you wind up with only a partial representation of what actually happened over the course of the concert experience. Furthermore, where you point your camera determines what ultimately "represents" the event; so you have to work very hard to ensure you're focusing your data collection on what's actually important.

The collection methods offered through digital analytics introduce the opportunity to take much larger samples (or even observe entire populations) more frequently (or even continually). But the nature of variety in digital data collection comes not only from the increased possibilities for sampling, but from the type of data collected through that sample.

Conversion data: Sales/transactions

Data about consumer's business-driving transactions is the core measure of Conversion Science — but access to this data differs substantially by the type of product offering.

Direct capture of conversion data is easy for physical retailers, digital retailers, and online direct to consumer (D2C) sellers of content, goods, or services. These D2C sales can take place through intermediaries like etsy.com or Amazon.com and still provide sales data directly to the seller. This data is typically connectable to details about the consumer. For offline sellers, that is accomplished through the direct nature of the sale, or a loyalty program link made at the point of sale; where everything associated with that buyer's purchase transaction can be tied to a unique profile for the buyer. And for online sellers, data about the buyer is collected directly, and their digital trail to the sale (for example, the referring sites or search terms that brought them in) can be linked to the transaction.

For wholesalers who are not directly selling their own goods such as consumer packaged goods (CPG) companies and manufacturers of all kinds — the story about sales begins with what is being shipped to retailers. When details about the end of that story (actual sales to consumers) become available, they are seldom provided directly from retailers, but more frequently come from sales data syndication services like Nielsen and IRI — delivered in batches and with some delay. And unlike the data about consumers, their paths to purchase and their purchase habits available to digital sales and retailers, the understanding of who has purchased and the context of their purchase available to wholesale industries is limited to bulk categorization and clustering of behaviors.

In short — the data about consumers and their purchasing behavior that is available to those who have direct engagement in making the sale is much better than data for those developing offerings to be sold through an intermediary. All data-driven communications strategies intended to be optimized toward sales must take the availability of sales data into account. For example, the understanding of what's working and what's not in communications to deliver a "return" on marketing spend is dependent on the ability to associate the audience that content is reaching with the purchase behaviors of that audience. When the description of sales outcomes does not provide granularity in the details of the audience, or the results of sales are delayed long past the point of contact with media, those associations become very difficult to establish. However, when sales can be linked to an actual contact with a consumer, as with digital marketing and sales, there is a very powerful ability to continually fine-tune communications to drive sales.

Operational and channel performance

Conversion data provides the ultimate measure of "return" on the delivery of conversion-seeking interfaces, content, and experiences. In determining a "return on investment" (ROI), our measure of "investment" comes from the collection of operational efforts and expenditures in the delivery of our interfaces, content, and experiences.

There is great variety within channel spend and performance data. Marketing that takes place in mass media like broadcast television or out of home advertising often requires investment months before the content will reach consumers. The operational spend data is captured in a budget line, and the channel key performance indicator (KPI) around this purchase is the planned number of impressions to consumers through the channels. Other spending — such as budgets for digital search, social and ad network static, interactive and video content delivery — is accrued as content is shown, with a specific cost paid (through an automated bidding system) for each impression. The operational channel metrics for this content will often look beyond impression and into behaviors including interaction with the content and click-through to a target destination. However, these behavioral metrics can only be assigned value when the causal relationships between interactions with content and eventual conversion are understood.

Beyond the marketing content and ad interfaces, consumers reach the offering's owned experience. Many "return on advertising investment" or "return on marketing investment" approaches only evaluate the performance of channels leading to the point of engagement or sale, but not the owned engagement itself. Whether the owned interface for engagement is an in-real-life (IRL) environment like a store, an informational website, or an e-commerce platform, there should be measurement of spend to drive sales and quality of consumer engagement, and the impact of these on the ultimate contribution to sales from the advertising and marketing that preceded it.

First party consumer data

Customer relationship management (CRM) databases hold records of individual consumers who have allowed their data to be collected. For any company transacting directly with consumers (or B2B buyers), the CRM database should hold details about everyone who has transacted with that company (and shared their information). It will also hold details about prospective customers to support sales and direct marketing efforts.

Wholesale marketers who do not transact directly with consumers will often still develop and maintain CRM databases of consumers who have opted in to receive information or other benefits from the marketer. The beverage maker Red Bull, for example, puts significant effort into giving consumers reasons to share information with them through the delivery or sponsorship of content and experiences. Much of their content is free, but even more content becomes accessible when consumers connect with them using a social profile or email. Likewise, Red Bull hosts or sponsors events ranging from music to dance to sports to food and culture, and participants in these events will likely opt-in to sharing their contact information with Red Bull. The content and experiential delivery has benefits in maintaining affinity for the product among consumers and maintaining its position as the top product in the category, but the information collected can also help Red Bull understand details about consumers that are typically owned by the retailers that sell Red Bull, but not Red Bull itself.

Unilever, the maker of over 400 brands, is recognized for its highly developed approach to CRM.

Unilever does not have to create opportunities to collect customer data; with 2.5 billion people using their products, the company maintains millions of inbound contacts on a continuous basis. While Red Bull's CRM holds records around consumers' interests in events and activities, Unilever's CRM is a source of insight into customer feedback on its 400 brands — both positive and negative — from all around the world. Not only does Unilever utilize CRM to establish direct communication around complaints or concerns and send appreciation for positive feedback, but it mines this source for immediate feedback on where systemic issues with a product or its marketing may be emerging, and it feeds CRM data through predictive models to identify emerging trends in its consumer base and their preferences.

Third party consumer data

Deciding what data about existing or targeted consumers should guide the content and media design for reaching and converting more prospective consumers is the primary premise of conversion science. As discussed, first party data provides insights into consumers and their direct engagement with your interfaces, content, and experiences. Direct sellers will be able to collect transactions within their individual-based first party data, while others will acquire transactional data around their offerings in bulk. Engagement with consumers will be collected with unique identifying data when in owned channels, and anonymously when served through advertising or social networks.

Third party data providers offer the opportunity to enrich owned first party data with information about those consumers that is not collected through your direct engagement with those consumers, and to apply that enriched data to subsequent targeting through methods such as "look-alike modeling", where targeting is focused on consumers who "look like" those who have transacted previously with your offering. And even if you don't have first party data to match against third party data providers' IDs, anyone can create "audiences" with these vendors and learn about the composition and behavior of consumers segmented by demographics, purchasing behavior, and engagement with all sorts of trackable content.

Third party data providers offer many opportunities for behavioral segmentation and targeting. For example, *location intelligence* providers like PlaceIQ and Factual track the movement of consumers' devices through the world, and can match the consumers you give them (as identifiable records for match back or general targeting criteria) to devices, then tell you where and when you can find consumers matching your criteria in physical locations (i.e. in transit, at stores, engaging in entertainment, dining out and socializing, or at home).

Clickstream aggregators like similar Web offer another angle on data about consumers that cannot be collected directly. Solutions like these utilize browser and app add-ons and their owned panels of consumers to track everything consumers are seeing and doing online — including searches, app usage, and activity within social networks. This adds critical data for understanding consumer's interests, exposure to messages, and behaviors beyond what can be learned from their engagement with only your interfaces and content.

Consumer data vendors help fill in remaining gaps about consumers — especially regarding their offline transactions and behaviors. Companies like Experian and Acxiom acquire and ingest data about consumers' transactions and behaviors in every area. These companies develop deep knowledge on a person-by-person basis, using a persistent unique ID to replace "personally identifying information" like name, address, and social security number. This information includes consumers' household composition, employment, income and credit, and how their money and time is spent; with breakdowns across all spending from utilities to healthcare, to food, housing, and clothing, to auto and other transportation, to education, travel, and entertainment. These companies know how frequently purchases are made, how many are made online and offline, and through which retailers purchases are made.

It is important to note that third party data providers will not sell information about the exact transactions for a specific consumer that is passed to them from CRM. Instead, they will send back classifications and ranges, indicating how frequently they buy certain things or exhibit certain behaviors, with ranges around levels of spend and engagement for example.

Customer Data Platforms

Integrating all of these data sources together, organizing them into existing and target consumer segments, and evaluating activation against these segments can be done on an ad hoc or as-needed basis, but sophisticated conversion science will establish a customer data platform (CDP) for these purposes.

The greatest benefit of a CDP is the removal of silos around consumer data through the organization, and the unification of data into rich "identity graphs" for consumers and consumer segments. Through the CDP, data from CRM can be merged with website and app data, which can be merged into media targeting and engagement data, which can be merged with transactions and third party location, clickstream, and consumer data. This single source of truth about consumer data can then be partitioned back out to the organization with silos imposed as needed.

Unilever again provides a best-in-class example of a CDP at work. To understand consumers of its 400 brands across the globe, Unilever has staffed over 20 "people data centers" around the globe to bring regional perspective to the insights in its CDP. The data in this platform spans from all of that CRM data, to primary research insights and social media monitoring, to media placement and response data with the incorporation of third party audience data, and finally to as much sales data as possible.

There are several objectives to all of this data collection that were shared by Unilever in its 2018 shareholder filings.

Brand and Marketing Investment is focused on maximizing return on spend. We are increasing spend in the areas driving growth, such as digital media and in-store, whilst reducing production and promotional spend.... We are creating more content in-house while making existing assets go further. Our 16 U-Studios in 13 countries create brand content faster and more efficiently than external agencies. Improvements to measurement and verification of digital audiences ensure we maximize value in digital advertising alongside improvements in the measurement of influencer follower data.

In these same reports to its shareholders and in other publicity it shares, Unilever touts its ambition to establish a billion one-to-one relationships with the consumers of its brands.

When Unilever speaks about areas driving growth, their model and ambition is informed by the success of their direct-to-consumer subscription-based Dollar Shave Club offering, and is being developed through other D2C offerings including Skinsei, a subscription service for personalized skin care, an online store and direct marketing for their Nexxus brand of haircare, a service in the UK called "Blow LTD" delivering styling services at home. And with the acquisition of Graze, a UK-based online D2C healthy snacking company that ships personalized orders to consumers, Unilever has turned the corner from D2C for personal care to D2C for food.

All of these D2C interfaces with consumers feed transactional information into Unilever's CDP, where it is merged and enriched with data from all the other sources mentioned above, and applied not just to optimizing marketing (creative and media placement) to these consumers (and their look-alike counterparts) across all of Unilever's other brands, but also to the development of new offerings through R&D efforts and new product introductions.

Velocity

Historically, data collected for analysis of consumers and their behaviors were collected in batches. Traditional market research involves the fielding of surveys or focus groups or ethnographic observation. Sales or transactions were collected at point of sale, then delivered periodically in bulk for analysis.

Digital engagement produces a more continuous stream of data. This "streaming" data challenges the insight generating mechanisms of traditional consumer insights and performance analysis that were built for processing batches of data delivered periodically.

This challenge is solved with the application of algorithmic computation to process the constant stream of data. Algorithms not only offer quicker application of traditional models, but also introduce new and perhaps better models for analysis depending on the question.

This rapid acceleration in the velocity of data and the shift in analytic methods required to process that continuous stream (and volume) of data also requires more than just minor adjustments in how consumer insights and performance analysis are applied to the delivery of interfaces, content, and experiences. These changes are precipitating a paradigm shift in the notion of how "market research" and "consumer insights" should be applied to guide engagement with the brand's relevant stakeholders to optimally serve the objectives of all involved parties. This paradigm shift in what analytics-driven experience design can and should be able to accomplish is a significant driver in the evolving and transformation of consumer engagement away from the 20th century marketing approach of outbound-directed message broadcasting into a more organic feedback system with capability to continually learn from inputs and adapt appropriately to increasingly broad arrays of context.

Volume

Undoubtedly, the amount of data a company like Unilever is ingesting into its CDP would be described as "big data". Smaller scale ventures engaging consumers with interfaces, content, and experiences may not produce as much data as Unilever, but if they're accessing all the data available to them, they will likely begin generating larger volumes of structured and unstructured data than ever before. As they do, it is lucky that the availability of scalable high-performance data structures has been productized by companies like Amazon and Google.

Ultimately, dealing with the challenge of volume is a technical problem of storage and retrieval. Understanding the basics of the solutions to these problems requires first understanding the two forms that data can take.

Structured data is any data that has components which can be consistently and uniformly categorized.

It would fit well into a spreadsheet, with every row a new record and a series of columns that each represent an element of the data, with a clear field type (numeric, date/time, string) for each element. Most data traditionally used for business — from CRM to spend to sales to primary research results — has been designed to live as structured data because of how easily it can be organized, retrieved, inter-connected, and analyzed.

Unstructured data has become much more prevalent as the data most commonly generated through digital media. Every written post or video or image posted on the web contains potentially valuable information for understanding the people we're trying to reach and convert. It can reveal their interests and dislikes. It can illustrate their level and pattern of engagement with our content, interfaces, and experiences. It can reveal their use of our offering or the offering of a competitor. But none of that information is delivered in a clearly categorized and organized way. Social media posts are not written into forms that decompose into fields like "rating of product" and "reasons for concern" and "relevant interests around use". Those insights may exist in all kinds of content shared through the web, but not in a nice structured format that provides 1 through 5 rankings around standardized questions, or standardized labels around the content of videos or images.

Addressing the volume of structured and unstructured data that can be collected once a focus is placed on developing data-driven insights requires technical expertise. Luckily for many organizations, the expertise of big-data-based business like Amazon and Google has been made available to everyone as yet another offering of these data-driven giants. Because they have very advanced scalable infrastructure in place for their own operations, it was a natural step for them to build a profit opportunity from what would otherwise be a cost center around their operations. We will not be concerned in these pages with the technical steps required to spin up data environments from a cloud storage provider. These are subscription-based services that price mainly around levels of use. They are built on the provisioning of "virtual machines" to subscribers — meaning that subscribers get data infrastructure over the web. They provide storage options for both structured and unstructured data. They offer security for data, and options to fine-tune security within your instances. When establishing a place for your data through one of these offerings, the primary considerations will often be pricing and speed, with the array of integrated services from each offering for processing and utilizing your data as an important secondary consideration.

The Fundamental Analytics Architecture: The Analytics Pyramid

There are technological challenges to collecting data that are increasing in volume, velocity, and variety, but there's a more fundamental concern that precedes dealing with what is collected; the determination of the data that should be collected in the first place and the ways in which it should be applied to experience delivery. These decisions will in turn determine the data management and experience delivery technologies required to achieve those results.

The first job of the conversion scientist is to determine their data requirements and communicate these through the organization. Without correctly defined data requirements, the conversion scientist will be working entirely or in part with incomplete and/or inaccurate data, limiting the capabilities of their analysis. Typically, any conversion scientist seeking to advance their efforts will find that they require more and better data to build more accurate models. In these cases, the conversion scientist's ability to communicate and ultimately "sell" the need to spend time and energy on data collection become critical. This ability to mobilize the organization around the collection and integration of more and better data begins with the establishment of a common organization understanding of the applications of data to business objectives.

"The Data Applications Pyramid", as shown in Figure 3.1, may be useful as a model around which this common understanding can be established.

Figure 3.1
Data
Applications
Pyramid

The Analytics Pyramid shown in Figure 3.1 segments the possible application of the insights derived from data and analysis into four layers: (1) Descriptive, (2) Predictive, (3) Prescriptive, and (4) Adaptive.

Descriptive Analytics

The foundational layer represents "Descriptive" analytics, and divides these into three sub-categories.

(1) Performance Analytics

This is the type of analysis most commonly envisioned when "analytics" is discussed, since performance insights are what most reporting and dashboard tools have been designed to deliver. In performance analytics, we find the "counts and amounts" related to KPIs within digital channels; things like impressions, page visits, bounce rate, open rate, click-through rate, likes, follows, views, and downloads.

Performance analytics tell us how we are doing in terms of *outputs,* but they do not tell us much about who is doing this thing or the context in which the thing occurs, and so are less immediately applicable to an understanding of actual business *outcomes.* This is exacerbated by the fact that performance metrics only measure the positive occurrences of a certain output, so in and of themselves they tell us absolutely nothing about an equally important set of data, all the cases in which the behavior *did not* occur — which is the understanding we'll need to improve performance. For that information, we turn from the "what" and "how much" of performance analytics to the "who, where, when, and why" of context analytics.

(2) Context Analytics

Good reports and dashboards present their performance analytics in context, because without context we have no basis to act on the insights around performance. If performance analytics tell us some KPI is underperforming our expectations, we have no basis for designing a fix to this issue until we understand whether this is true for everyone or just certain types of people, whether it happens all the time or just at specific times, whether there is a pattern of behavior that appears before and/or after the occurrence (or equally important, the non-occurrence) that might indicate a possible point of intervention to increase the desired behavior. Thus, contextual analytics like segmentation and path analysis give us more clarity around performance.

Unfortunately, not all reports and dashboards are good reports and dashboards. In fact, the vast majority of descriptive analysis provided for marketing in organizations is provided as performance data without much context.

To a large degree, this is due to the lack of descriptive data available around most KPIs. The collection of data from many channels has been implemented haphazardly, often as an afterthought, and often on a tiny budget. In part, this is due to the old paradigm of outbound mass marketing in which marketing managers did not understand how data could be used to guide their practice. Data was seen as simply a means for proving the success of what they designed through traditional market research, design, and management approaches. Some data was better than no data, but all the data really needed to do was prove that marketing was working.

Now, measuring whether marketing is working is not
enough, especially when it does not appear to be
working. Now, the reason that something works or
doesn't has become of great interest. Now, marketing managers are suddenly asking about the data
they have accessible to explain the performance they
are getting from across all of their marketing channels. And they're finding that data doesn't exist, so
they're turning to the readers of this book to bring
it into being. Establishing contextual insights to
explain performance is the first place to start.

(3) Research

The third sub-segment in descriptive analytics is marketing research. Performance analytics rightly holds
the prominent first position in digital analytics; if we
are doing nothing else, we should at least be measuring performance. The performance we observe is
contextualized and better understood through the
introduction of contexts like segmentation and pathing, but performance does not become explained
(particularly in a statistically valid sense) until
research methods are introduced.

The most basic type of research that should be conducted around digitally collected data is the development and maintenance of descriptive statistics
around key performance indicators, particularly
measures of centrality (mean, median, and mode)
and measures of dispersion (variance and standard
deviation). These basic statistical measures allow us
to define statistical "norms" around our performance variables, and are best when defined for multiple contexts, particularly segments. Segmentation
itself around digitally collected variables falls into
this research category, as does basic correlation to

test the significance of various steps throughout the path analysis.

Observations about drivers of performance collected through all of the descriptive methods should be defined as *hypotheses* which may then be tested in the research function to develop evidence about the drivers of performance. And often, the data that have been collected to a point of decision making are not applicable to the new question that is seeking an answer. New data can be generated through testing.

The benefit of testing and optimization analytics is that it relieves management of the requirement to place big bets on just one square and run the risk of guessing wrong. The hypotheses they test may be developed from the data they have through descriptive analytics, but the data on which they ultimately base their decision will emerge from a carefully conducted approach to developing prescriptive analytics.

Predictive Analytics

The insights we develop through our descriptive analytics will result in the emergence of observed and or tested "rules" around certain outcomes. For example, through observation it may emerge that people in Segment A tend to move with higher success from the consideration to the purchase stage of their decision process after viewing a type of video, and that a reminder email to those who did not convert during the visit in which they watched the video can prompt a large number of those to return and convert.

We may find that for those who have not received an email, a Facebook post showing the product they viewed is the right method for prompting a higher than average return for conversion. We may have tested various periods of time to wait before sending the email or Facebook post and established sub-segmentation for (1) those for whom a reminder in 1–2 days is most effective, (2) those for whom a second reminder is effective, and (3) those who were apparently not as interested in converting as their view of the video suggested under our initial model.

The understanding of these "rules" in all of their specific contexts provides the basis for the development of predictive models. These rules may be applied as the training dataset for planning and forecasting, offering relevant data to ROI forecasts and other predictive performance models. They may also be codified into the "programmatic" delivery of the marketing experience through tools such as demand side platforms (DSPs), programmatic media buying, and marketing automation software. In each of these platforms, the "general rule" for the best approach to drive any user through to a conversion is established from the data and coded to be followed whenever a user matching the right criteria appears in the right circumstances.

Following our example above, if the system recognizes that a visitor to the landing page belongs to Segment A, it will programmatically fill a prominent spot on the page with the right kind of video. Our data collection should record if the video was watched, and whether the call-to-action (CTA) to convert was then followed. If the visitor did not convert in that session, the Marketing Automation system will begin the countdown to the follow-up contact, will identify whether the follow-up will be through email or Facebook, will send then appropriate follow-up at the appropriate time, will record whether the desired outcome occurred, and will proceed to the appropriate next step.

Everything that occurred above was based on a series of predictions about the best next step to drive to an outcome, and the basis for those predictions is the data collected through our descriptive and prescriptive processes. Through the technologies described, marketing scientists may now predefine a staggeringly large set of step-by-step rules to be followed under an equally large set of circumstances for any number of types of digital users.

The limitation on the application of predictive analytics to drive optimal marketing delivery is not one of models or technology — these exist. The limitations are with data. If marketers do not have sufficient contextual insight, research into segments and paths, and tested hypotheses about previously untried approaches, the predictions about what is best to do next in any given case will be developed from an incomplete understanding of the problem and all possible solutions, and as such, may predict a "best" path that misses better alternatives. Good predictive modeling requires contextualization of performance around the target objective, and good research into segmentation and the paths of those segments from point to point through their engagement with the brand.

Feeding historical data into a tool that will act autonomously against predictions it makes from that data can be a benefit to the business when the data is good and the predictions are accurate, or it can be an autopilot system that drives marketing results straight into the side of a mountain through a series of bad decisions built on the rules it established from the data it was given. In other words, conversion scientists should seek to build predictive, programmatic marketing around as many decisions as the data warrant, but the limits of the data should be well understood, and efforts to extend the limits of the data should be recognized as an ongoing pursuit. This pursuit involves a constant cycling of the results from predictive delivery back into the front-end of the descriptive process, to proceed through contextualization, research, and testing to a new set of improved predictions.

Prescriptive Analytics

At some point in efforts at data-driven planning, we will find ourselves developing an engagement strategy that involves trying something for which there is no prior example, and thus no prior measurement. For example, a new segment may develop, or a new channel for communication may emerge, or a new context for engagement may evolve. These new conditions will require the development of new strategies.

Research and testing should be conducted to understand more about the new situation, and this research may reveal similarities that allow us to use past performance data to guide the new strategy. However, given that we will be trying something that has not been tried before, our predictive analytics from such data will be directional at best.

When it is possible to develop predictive models based on small data or data that seems similar to the case at hand are possible, what's really happening in these cases is not predictive analysis, but prescriptive analysis. Predictive analytics are based on observation of *what* is involved as the inputs to generating a measured outcome, and by *how much* of each of those inputs influences the outcome.

Prescriptive analytics simply adds the question of "why" to the "what" and "how much" of predictive analytics. The need for prescriptive analytics is reached when the data in our possession explain a past that is different from the future we expect, or have not accrued enough information to clearly establish predictions around cause and effect. When the mechanics around "what drove results" and "how much" in the past are from a situation that is different from what we are facing moving forward, or when there is not enough data from the past about our situation to effectively define how much change is produced over time, what we can turn to instead is insight around "why" the inputs have tracked the results we have measured.

The questioning of "why" in our analysis allows us to move beyond the observed volumes of inputs and outputs in a path of cause and effect to develop ideas (and gather data) about why the inputs we're measuring occur at the frequencies we observe. This may lead us to think more about how inputs look different for different types of people, or when circumstances around the inputs change. Such additional questions may help us collect new data, and will let us evaluate whether changes in how inputs are presented could change their frequency in association with an outcome, which ultimately helps us prescribe how alternative inputs might lead to different results in outcomes.

Adaptive Analytics

Adaptive analytics is an extension of predictive and prescriptive analytics, with the chief distinction being the application of "artificial intelligence" to drive the adaptive delivery of digital experiences. Machine learning algorithms are used in predictive and prescriptive analytics, and with each new data point, they automatically and continuously refine and diversify those models to deliver better predictions around ever-increasing specific contexts. With artificial intelligence, the "rules" that emerge from these predictions can be dynamically applied to delivery, and the data that comes back from the algorithmically defined actions then become a new source of data to drive further decisions — creating a feedback loop.

When this more fluid and adaptive form of delivery and analysis is coupled with integrated data, common customer segmentation, strong content management capabilities, programmatic delivery capabilities in marketing touch-points and sound marketing strategy, the stage is set for highly effective "real-time", "personalized", and "1 to 1" marketing. However, the climb up the analytics pyramid is not an easy journey; it must be approached deliberately and systematically.

Chapter FOUR

The Rush is on: Planning to Collect and Connect

4.1 Applied Conversion Analytics Playbook

The Applied Conversion Analytics Playbook (ACAP) is a template that guides a deliberate and systematic journey up the analytics pyramid and can serve as the core piece of documentation at the heart of every conversion science initiative. The ACAP allows the conversion science analyst to clearly identify the problems that data can solve, to identify the existing and needed sources of data to solve those problems, and to deliberately design the collection, organization, and application of the required data to experience delivery and to the evaluation of the results of that delivery.

The ACAP is built around four sections: (1) Problem Definition, (2) Solution Definition, (3) Data Design, and (4) Analytics Plan. These four sections together are designed to support communication and collaboration across multiple constituencies as both a strategic business communication and a conversion science engineering plan. This chapter will take a detailed look at the ACAP. An ACAP template is available at this book's counterpart website (www. architectingexperience.com).

4.2 ACAP Section One: Problem Definition

Business Problem/Business Case

The first section of the ACAP is focused on the definition of the business problem, on making the case for spending the business' time and money to solve the problem, and on documenting the measurable business objectives and key performance indicators (KPIs) associated with the successful fulfillment of the business case.

The fundamental problem the conversion scientist will want to answer for any type of offering is the question of how to increase conversions. This question typically breaks down into more granular concerns, such as "how to reach the people we think will convert", "how to increase the probability they will convert", "how to keep them from leaving after conversion", and "how to win back those who have left". The business problem statement in the ACAP should articulate a problem around one or more of these questions that can be solved by the application of data to interfaces, content, and experience and quantify the potential value of that solution.

Sample Business Problem

Icculus Industries produces musical instruments. The U.S. market for guitars and percussion instruments is estimated at over $2 billion dollars annually. Icculus Industries seeks to expand its share of this opportunity with a new line of custom 3D printed guitars and percussive instruments. To justify scaling its investment in this line, in its first year, Icculus is seeking to sell 12,000 units for an average unit price of $125.

    To achieve these sales, Icculus Industries needs to: (1) reach guitar and percussion shoppers to create

*awareness of these products, (2) educate consumers about
the benefits of a custom 3D printed instrument, (3) enable
easy online purchase, and (4) provide excellent customer
experience after the instrument has been delivered to
increase referral and repeat purchases.*

Business Objectives & Key Performance Indicators

Once we have established clear documentation of
the business problem and the benefit that will come
from solving the problem, we can then turn our
focus to the definition of solutions. Accordingly, the
next section of the ACAP is devoted to the documentation of objectives and KPIs for the business in general and marketing in specific.

Objectives & Key Performance Indicators

Each of the problems defined should be given a
matching **objective**. These objectives simply describe
what we intend to accomplish to resolve the associated problem. Objectives should be stated in terms
that will allow them to be measured for performance. The measurement of performance against
these objectives is conducted through **KPIs**.

Considering the business problem defined in the
sections above, our associated objectives and KPIs
might look like this:

Business Objective 1: *Reach guitar and percussion
shoppers to create awareness of these products.* **KPIs:**
(1) Number of target consumers seeing our content
(reach). (2) Number of times consumers are exposed

to our content (frequency). (3) Cost per thousand views of that content. (4) Engagement with that content (full video plays, click-throughs, social likes, and shares). (5) Increased traffic to site.

Business Objective 2: *Educate consumers about the benefits of a custom 3D printed instrument.* **KPIs:** (1) Engagement with educational content (full video plays, click-throughs, social likes, and shares). (2) Increased traffic to site to view content. (3) Subscription to content sources.

Business Objective 3: *Enable easy online purchase.* **KPIs:** (1) Site visitors starting purchase. (2) Site visitors completing purchase. (3) Number of sales and value of sales.

4.3 ACAP Section Two: Consumer-centered Solutions

The second section of the ACAP turns our focus from describing the problems we are going to solve (**what**) and the reasons behind them (**why**) to now define more specifically for **whom** we will be solving these problems and **when** and **where** they will be solved. This is the section of the ACAP that is most closely aligned with consumer-centered strategy, user experience, and design disciplines.

Our understanding of prospective and existing customers and the solutions we build for them are based on data. Figure 4.1 shows how data are drawn into and out of consumer-centered solution design.

At the top of the cycle depicted in Figure 4.1, data about conversion performance with consumers

Figure 4.1 |
The Data-
centered
Design Cycle |

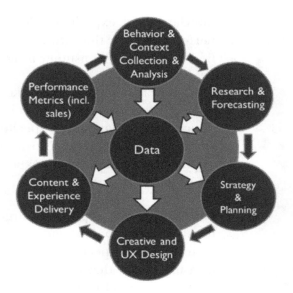

as well as consumer demographics, behaviors, and contexts are evaluated for the insights they give us on consumers.

Whenever we want to try something new, it may turn out that there's been no data captured in what we've done before to help us evaluate the expected results of what we're trying to do. So in the next step clockwise, we conduct any research required to help further develop the insights needed for the interfaces, content, and experiences we are planning to build. With all the data and insights we need in hand, we are also able to develop forecasting models to develop expectations about what our proposed new approaches can accomplish, and thus what should be spent to achieve them.

Proceeding clockwise, strategy and planning define the possible approaches to be developed in content, interface, and experience delivery to improve on performance for the various consumer types identified through our consumer insights.

Our conversion strategies, backed by data and forecasted expectations, move next into creative and UX design, where data about specific characteristics of customers and their Jobs to be Done are critically important to build relevant experiences that provide highly effective results.

Finally, data are applied to target and personalize the delivery of content and experience, and to complete the cycle, performance of that experience is measured, with that performance data defining the next stage areas for optimization, which will in turn determine new data collection and research needs to begin the cycle again.

The second section of the ACAP is where we explicitly design the "solution" to our defined problems by describing the digital experience we plan to deliver. As shown in Figure 4.1, the definition of user experience must be guided by data. Therefore, this second section of the ACAP is designed to guide and document our thinking about the integration between data and user experience design and delivery.

Inductive and Deductive Analysis

Because analysis is required to make sense of data that drives our conversion-oriented designs into delivery, before getting into more detailed descriptions and examples of the process for designing solutions, it is worth discussing the two different fundamental approaches to conducting analysis.

Inductive analysis begins with a pool of data and no theory about what insights might be contained within the data. The analyst assesses the data in an attempt to "induce" a theory from the data.

Deductive analysis on the contrary begins with a theory to be tested — a hypothesis. In this case, the analyst assesses the data to identify whether — and if so how strongly — the theory is supported by evidence.

Since the first step in our solution design process is to define more than one segment of consumers in a way that lets us more effectively target our efforts to convert consumers through content and media, we will look at these two different analytic methods around that objective.

The inductive approach to defining segments will take all the data we have on consumers from something like a Consumer Data Platform and mine it with the hope that classifications of different types of people will emerge from the data. For example, developing "clusters" around average levels of one or more measured variables is a common inductive approach, so running the data through a K-means clustering algorithm would be a common first step. A K-means clustering algorithm can be told how many clusters to make within a set of data and will group all of the data into that number of clusters using their statistical distance from one another around some key value. So we might take data we have about our customers' frequency of spending — which in the case of our example could be how often they buy a new instrument — and have a K-means algorithm find some number of clusters around that frequency variable. From that, we could dig into the data from any of those "frequency segments" clusters and look at any of the other variables we have for those consumers. In the case of our example, we would be seeking insights that would help us understand what can get their attention and address their jobs to be done.

The deductive approach to defining segments will begin with a hypothesis about different types of people. In our case, this will be around the different jobs to be done we believe people might have. It is often helpful to have some higher level classification of people to think through, so starting a deductive approach from the results of an inductive classification can be a good start. In this case, let's assume we've established clusters around types of instruments bought and frequency of purchase around those types. We've mined the other variables describing these consumers, which provide us with information about the demographics of these groups, but not as much as we'd like about their interests and attitudes.

Looking into the frequency and types of purchase and the demographics of this group can lead us to develop theories about what motivates these consumers to buy. In the scientific approach, these theories become hypothesis which we can develop as we add data, and then we finally test and refine them further to bring them closer and closer to the truth. Research is an important means to collect additional data to support hypotheses about consumer's motivations, attitudes, and intentions, as is the design of behavioral data collection into more points of engagement that we have with the consumer.

Each of these approaches has benefits and limits. Inductive analysis can only be built on data we have — so the insights into what types of people there are result entirely from what we've learned about people to that point. Inductive analysis will allow us to find real differences between people in the data we have, but it will not allow us to firmly establish an understanding of people that isn't drawn from what we've already learned about them. Deductive analysis begins with a theory or hypothesis about what types of people there are — and so can propose that there are segments built around variables we may not yet have measured. But deductive analysis does not give us definitive confirmation of our theories until we've collected data to support the theory and tested our assumptions against the data. The limitations of each method can be overcome when they are used together to develop insights about our targets for conversion.

Analytic Methods: Clusters, Factors, and Correlation

Chapter 3 introduced a variety of data sources about consumers, from first-party transactional and behavioral data to third-party consumer profile enrichment that can and should be applied in understanding consumers as we design and deliver experiences. As we step into ACAP's section on solutions, our understanding of who consumers are and what needs to be solved for them will come through inductive and deductive uses of data.

Our first step in understanding consumers is applying inductive analysis to find patterns in the information we have about them. To make our example simple, we will imagine a CRM dataset for Icculus Industries collected through opt-in sign-up. We have names, addresses, phone and email, records of engagement with our website including search terms for entry and sources of referral where applicable, and purchase history where applicable (since some signed-up at purchase and some signed-up while browsing the site). We also asked a few optional questions about occupation, level of musical ability, and interests during the sign-up process and have this information for half of our dataset. These are all data that any organization with a website, a CRM system, and a well-designed data collection plan can collect for just the cost of that technology.

If we are interested in enriching these data, we can pay a service like Acxiom to match our records with information they have about the consumers in our CRM (via personally identifiable information — or PII — like name, address, and email) and send us back an anonymized dataset providing more variables about our consumers. When these data reappear, all the PII will be removed and replaced with classifications related to each consumer. Age, gender, and geography will replace the PII we had for name and address, but we will have added new information like household income, purchase behaviors, media engagement behaviors, and attitudes and beliefs. While we won't have these linked to specific consumers as the data are anonymized, we will have enriched data about the composition of our CRM database and an ability to find frequencies and other patterns in that data.

Our first question in conducting analysis is whether we are evaluating common and unique attributes of consumers in isolation of outcomes or trying to understand consumer attributes in terms of an outcome.

In the first case, our analysis is about dividing our data into smaller groups, or "classes", so we will apply classification models. In the second case, we are seeking to show the relationship between an outcome and its dependency on inputs, so we will apply measures of "correlation" to show the co-relationship between a dependent outcome and the independent inputs to that outcome.

Clusters

Classification approaches will be conducted by the statisticians or data science practitioners in your organization. One of the most common and rudimentary classification techniques is the "clustering" of cases based on their similarity to one another. With a method called K-means clustering, K is the number of clusters we want to create. Since addressing segments in unique ways requires investing time and resources for design and delivery to each segment, we will typically want to keep our K relatively small.

Icculus Industries is interested in creating a group for those who are most likely to buy innovative products, those who are moderately likely, and those who are least likely. K-means clustering for $K = 3$ would find three "averages" in the data for dollars spent on a certain type of "innovative" product and would group the whole dataset around those averages.

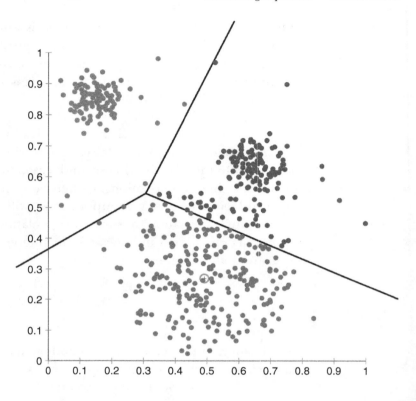

Figure 4.2
K-means
Cluster Plot

Clustering has the benefit of identifying how well lines can be drawn around consumers based on certain variables (see Figure 4.2). However, while clustering establishes the level of distinction we can make between consumers, it does not help us understand what elements of those differences will be most relevant to the results we're seeking. Knowing that we have three distinct groupings of low, medium, and high dollars spent on new products for our consumers relative to each other does not tell us what this means for our content objectives. What is causing consumers to spend on these types of products and can we influence those causes?

Factors

The next thing we'll ask of the statisticians or data science practitioners in our organization is an understanding of what variables matter within our data. Factor analysis allows us to evaluate the relationship between variables or factors in our data. For Icculus Industries, we've established groups within our existing customer base around levels of purchase relative to each other. Factor analysis can tell us how much the related information we know about our consumers are associated with each other and are thus likely related through an unmeasured but still real and impactful fact about consumers.

From among our high-purchase cluster, let's evaluate the occupations, incomes, and interests in sound, style, and uniqueness of instruments as reported through customer surveys.

Variables	Factor 1	Factor 2
Occupation	0.68	0.19
Sound	0.56	0.27
Income	0.19	0.61
Style	0.38	0.42
Unique	0.11	0.55

In the table provided, factor analysis shows us two factors, or underlying facts about consumers that are reflected in what we can measure. The "Factor 1" column shows high "factor loading" for "occupation" and a survey response to the importance of sound quality. It also shows that interest in style is somewhat important but that income and an interest in uniqueness of a product are not strong indicators of our first underlying consumer factor.

The "Factor 2" column indicates an underlying fact about consumers around which income does matter, along with uniqueness and style, but occupation does not.

It is left to us to interpret and describe what underlying variables are implied by factor loading. These results seem to indicate that one factor of purchase in our high consumer base is independent of income but very dependent on occupation and sound. A quick look into occupation shows that many of these work in music as musicians or recording engineers. Thus, "music professional" is clearly one factor in buying, and we know that professional musicians value sound to a great extent. The other factor establishes that income and the uniqueness of the instrument underlie a fact about consumers. This implies a different motivation to purchase using disposable income — potentially as a collector. Do these results imply that among our top purchasers we have two groups — one of professionals and one of collectors? If so, we'd be nearing sub-segmentation within purchase-based clusters around different jobs to be done.

Correlation

Factor analysis has given us a sense of the statistical relationships between variables — defining which of them tend to occur together. This is an example of "correlation" — the statistical measure of the co-relationship of two or more variables.

The correlation of two variables can be positive, meaning that when one increases so does the other, or negative, meaning that when one increases the other declines.

Linear regression is a common approach to evaluating the correlation between a variable that we believe is influenced by other variables (this is called the dependent variable) and the variables that we believe do the influencing (these are the independent variables). For example, following our factor analysis, we might segregate all high-valued purchases of people who are involved in the music field and — for everyone who is left — evaluate how purchasing behavior varies with changes in income, uniqueness of product, and style of product.

A multivariate regression of income, style, and uniqueness of products bought against dollars spent last year in MS Excel returns the following table of coefficients and *p*-values.

	Coefficients	*p*-Value
Intercept	33.34126	0.001000
Income	81.28294	0.013709
Style	26.02530	0.049808
Unique	71.10057	0.002434

The intercept gives us an estimate for average sales if the other variables were not present. The other coefficients tell us how much that variable moves together with the intercept. In the results above, income and dollars spent are the most correlated; when one increases, so does the other. Style and dollars spent increase together only slightly, but uniqueness of product and dollars spent increase together almost as much as income. The *p*-value for each variable is the outcome of a statistical test. A *p*-value above 0.05 would mean there is at least a 5% chance that our results are an error and the actual coefficient is zero. In statistics, even a 5% chance of such an error is unacceptable. Because our *p*-values here are all lower than 0.05, we can accept this explanation of the relationship between each variable and the dollars spent.

This regression has perhaps helped us theorize that when dealing with the non-professional musician, or "collector" segment of our consumer base, as their income and the uniqueness of the product they are buying increases, so does the amount they spend with us. This is a useful insight to add to our consumer profiles, but we have to remember that while this correlation measurement establishes the shared change between these variables, it does not establish the direction of the dynamic or the cause and effect between them. At this point, cause and effect in this case is still just theory, and to establish cause and effect, we will need to conduct research or testing explicitly designed to provide that insight.

Research Methods

As mentioned in Chapter 3, the most common data used in the design of interfaces, content, and experience comes from smaller scale qualitative research that measures behavioral and attitudinal response through surveys, interviews, focus groups, and observation.

Qualitative Research

Research can be conducted to develop qualitative or quantitative insights. Qualitative research is meant to uncover certain qualities of what we are studying from among a small sample of individuals who meet certain criteria. Qualitative research is intended to elicit multiple and often specific perspectives on the questions we are researching but is not intended to show that those perspectives are statistically representative of our entire market. Qualitative research gives us insights from interviews, focus groups, or observation and participation with consumers that allow us to create better hypothetical starting points for thinking about how the entirety of our market might work — but it does not give us statistical confidence that we understand how all of our consumers will think or behave.

In terms of Icculus Industries, we had a theory that when dealing with the non-professional musician, or "collector" segment of our consumer base, their income and the uniqueness of the product they are buying determines the amount they spend with us. Qualitative research could involve a focus group of these non-professional musicians that would dig deeper into this theory, exploring what they feel makes something unique and the aspect that is valuable. We might also venture into those markets where products similar to ours are used in order to observe and understand the Jobs to be Done that are being solved effectively, and more importantly, those that have a much better scope of being solved. Such observation often reveals insights that were never considered in other research studies. For example, in our hypothetical case, we might observe that sometimes the buyer of unique instruments is not the "hobbyist", but instead a family member who buys these items as a gift.

Quantitative Research

Quantitative research is intended to provide statistical confidence around the attitudes and behaviors we can expect from the groups that we've researched. In this research, we seek answers that we can process numerically, so we ask and evaluate "how much", "how many", "how often", and "please rank on a scale" types of questions. The people we ask are our "sample" of a "population" — where the population is everyone in our target. Confidence means an ability to say "we are 95% sure that the results we have from our research would be seen for any randomly selected group for this population we're studying — and thus reflect the population as a whole" and that "in reality the percentages or probabilities we'd see around those attitudes and behaviors in the population will have only small variation from what's reported here." Put more concisely, statistical confidence means we'd get the same results over and over again when studying the same population.

Quantitative research is most commonly conducted via survey questionnaire. Surveys require enough response to be representative of our population with the degree of confidence mentioned above. The sample size formula and many calculators for sample size can be easily found online, and you'll find that a sample of around 400 people will usually be sufficient to represent the differences that could be found between even very large populations. A word of caution — as soon as an initial group of 400 is divided by some finding of difference among them, the results you might then find and claim as isolated within one of the subgroups may no longer have statistical significance against that sub-population if your sample for that subgroup has been reduced by the initial segmentation. So larger initial samples provide better opportunity for segmentation.

In terms of Icculus Industries' current question, quantitative research could involve a survey of existing customers (using our CRM), which could be evaluated by the type of customer (professional versus hobbyist). Here, we might ask both professionals and hobbyists about the different motivations for purchase and about the rank in importance of features. We could also sample people who aren't in our CRM but who have purchased a musical instrument or accessory in the last 6 months. Here, we would first ask about their relationship to playing (i.e. "professional", "semi-professional", "hobby") and then solicit the same insights into importance of features and motivations for purchase.

In our hypothetical case for Icculus Industries, at the end of our qualitative research, we will have counts and ranks of what matters to different types of consumers. We might also have learned that a third group should be considered between "professional" and "hobbyist" — a semi-professional who is not primarily occupied in music, but who treats music as a second profession and who performs or records for the public, irrespective of whether the person is compensated or not.

Consumer Insights

With all of our data collected, analysis conducted, and findings established, ACAP's section on behavioral and contextual insights is where we will define the customers we are seeking to engage through our digital experience as we've come to understand them. The objective of this section is to develop two or more segments based on characteristics about consumers' contexts and behaviors that will guide distinctive content and media targeting.

Insights into consumers are often built on such limited data that they tend to paint pictures in broad strokes, such as "millennials", or the classic "soccer mom" who raised those millennials (e.g. *A middle-class woman aged 29–40 focused on her children. Drives them everywhere. Has little time. Makes online purchases from our category weekly.*). Such broad-stroke descriptions clearly do not give interface, content, and experience design teams much to work with.

On the contrary, when customer insight research and digital data collection have been designed to provide Jobs to be Done insights in the context of consumers' interests, attitudes, and behaviors and we can place all of that in the context of different demographic and transactional groupings, then we have the right ingredients for comprehensive and fully fleshed personas that will actually let us "know" the people for whom we are building experiences through our marketing touch-points. Segments built from the more complete and complex understanding of customers that would have been developed through our methods discussed above will allow conversion-focused teams to better understand the people for whom they are designing content and experiences, which in turn will make way for better outcomes.

Some examples in terms of Icculus Industries' new 3D instruments offering are follows:

Sonic Innovators: Semi-professional and professional musicians, engineers, or producers who are seeking to bring new and unique elements into their recording process. *Demographics, transactional profile, and target share of sales inserted here.* JTBD hypothesis: Will value sound over style.

Showcasers: Semi-professional and professional musicians who consider the instruments they use to be part of the show. *Demographics, transactional profile, and target share of sales inserted here.* JTBD hypothesis: Will value visual appeal/style.

Collectors & Co.: Amateur and semi-professional musicians (and those who buy gifts for them) who seek new and unique "toys" to add to their collection. *Demographics, transactional profile, and target share of sales inserted here.* JTBD hypothesis: Will value unique and limited-edition items.

These profiles (in a more detailed form with reference to the research) will give the experience design team a clear understanding of several different types of customers, their motivations and interests, and their problems with the brand's experience. The value to addressing these motivations, interests, and problems is established through data-driven insights into demographic size and composition of the audience, the share of market for the group, and the targeted contribution of the group to growth. As a next step, the content and experience design team will now need to address the consumer's journey from initial awareness to eventual conversion.

Consumer Experience Mapping

As introduced in Chapter 2, a consumer's perception about the best solution for their jobs to be done will evolve throughout their experience leading up to conversion. Our chance of being the preferred solution at the end of this journey is improved when we understand how to stay engaged with the consumer throughout their journey. This understanding is best developed and documented through a "map" of the points of interface we can have with consumers as they move through their Consumer Decision Journey and the paths the journey can take from each of those steps, along with a general definition of how data can be collected and applied to enrich their experience with us at each point of connection.

The more detail an experience map includes, the more complex it will appear. Experience maps should strive for a comprehensive description of the paths a consumer can take in engaging with the brand through their journey with the understanding that experience maps are engineering diagrams not executive summaries and are not meant to be read at a glance.

Segment: Sonic Innovators

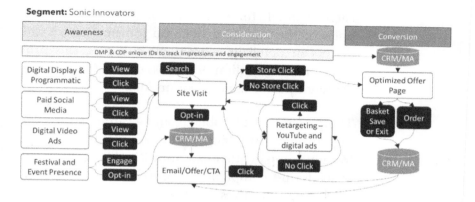

As we document the decision journey for each segment, we define the touch-points that will potentially be engaged throughout each step of the journey. With this experience map, we will subsequently be able to design each creative and user experience asset with a specific (or set of specific) customer segment/persona + stage + channel combination. Therefore, the experience map is a critical input for the methodological alignment of every component of the experience with a specific segment and their journey toward conversion.

By enforcing the methodological alignment of every component of the digital marketing experience with a specific segment at a specific point in the journey, marketing management requires that the basis for creative and UX design decisions be based on the formation of hypotheses about what will best deliver movement from each step toward the conversion goal at the end of the journey. By enforcing the definition of measurable KPIs against each of these objectives, marketing management articulates what kind of results the company should be seeing from

each channel, for each type of customer, at each
stage of the customer decision journey. As we will
discuss in detail in subsequent chapters, this provides the foundation for cross-channel customer-
centered performance measurement.

The generation of publicity and awareness through
high-profile advertising is a fine marketing objective
for any company that can afford it. The generation
of leads and completion of purchases are also fine
marketing objectives. With any marketing objective
(and business objective and customer objective),
what we want most from our objectives is that they
are explicitly defined and documented and that they
have an associated set of KPIs to guide their measurement. This book does not argue that every marketing activity should be measurable in terms of
revenue and ROI, but it does unquestionably argue
that *every marketing activity should be measurable,* since
ultimately there can be no truly effective management without measurement. By requiring that creative decisions are based in clearly articulated
hypotheses about what makes them effective in specific contexts and by defining the KPIs that determine effectiveness, marketing managers are well on
their way to being able to deliver not just optimal
channel mixes but also optimal content through
those channels.

With the measurement of performance against clear
journey-based objectives available to marketers,
there is absolutely no reason that hunches, guesses,
or opinions should ever be the primary basis for how
we engage with consumers. Thanks to measurement
designed against the expectations of a consumer
journey, we will be able to continue and expand on

interfaces and content that are working and stop allocating budget and exerting effort on those that aren't working.

Not only are there data available to provide data-driven guidance or direction at the start of any decision-making process but also there are even more data available around the performance resulting from prior decisions and around the options available to either extend positive results or fix negative results. The benefits of objectives-oriented creative production ensure that the creative, content, and overall user experience has been designed to deliver measurable results against clearly defined objectives. Because we know what to measure and have expectations around the results, through real-time measurement we are able to identify issues with the experience as they arise, and we are able to quickly develop and apply new hypotheses about what will improve performance.

ACAP Part One Summary

The first half of the Applied Digital Analytics Plan is focused on carefully and comprehensively articulating our objectives and applying data to give us insights that can drive success in these objectives. Without this important first step, we will not have a clear and common organizational understanding of what we should be measuring and analyzing, and our approach to data collection may be haphazard, siloed, and inconsistent across channels. This first half of the ACAP is where we are able to make a compelling business case for a program of data collection and analysis, grounding that case in a discussion of the business objectives we can meet through our improved approach to conversion science and analytics.

Before discussing the second half of the ACAP, which focuses on design of our data and the repositories and the specific ways in which we apply that data to experience delivery, the chapters that follow will discuss the ideal application of communications platforms, content strategy and data collection, analysis and experience delivery for businesses of all sizes. As we conclude this chapter, it is important to recognize that an organization's capability to reach the ideal applications of data and technology that you will read about will very much depend on the extent to which they have gone through the strategic thinking and collective articulation of customers and their objectives, digital experience vision, and business and marketing goals as outlined in the first half of the ACAP.

Chapter FIVE

Consumer Attention: The Brass Ring on the Media-Go-Round

Having established actionable consumer insights and aligned them against business objectives and a consumer experience map that anticipates the various contexts and mindsets through which we will engage consumers, we are now ready to turn to our next step in stage "1. Planning and Content Design" — the development of a creative platform designed to generate salience (attention) and resonance (from recall to engagement) with consumers (Figure 5.1).

As discussed back in the "Attention Economy" section of Chapter 2, successfully conveying the distinctive value of an offering to drive consumer behavior requires first capturing the attention of consumers so that they even see and register the offering. Recognizing an offering is the first step to eventually associating with it as a possible solution to a JTBD.

In our world of ever-present content competing for attention at every moment a consumer is engaged with media, the ability for content of any type to capture attention and establish awareness is a significant

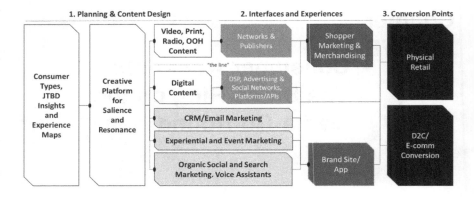

Figure 5.1
Planning and
Content Design

challenge. The mechanics for creating attention and awareness are relatively straightforward:

1. The content itself must earn attention through an appeal to consumers' senses.
2. The attention-earning content must make the effort to reach the target consumers often enough to increase its chances of becoming registered in their minds.

This chapter will explain the principles of designing content that is optimized for salience and resonance in the contexts of general design principles, and the specific insights provided through consumer insights and experience maps. Chapter 6 will then move us forward into the application of media to reach target consumers.

5.1 Salience: Earning Attention

Simply defined, attention is a state of concentration on information or content. Information surrounds each of us; as you read this there are all kinds of things to look at or watch in the space around you, there is the sound of your surrounding environment, and there are thoughts that may just jump into your head. These are all competing for your attention — and your attention goes wherever your concentration is placed.

The objective of any content is to capture the consumer's concentration from among everything the consumer could be focused on in that moment. The challenge increases with the volume of content or information that is also vying for that consumer's concentration in that moment.

Perceptual Stimuli: Appeals to the Senses

Attention first requires a successful appeal to the senses. For mediated content, this is limited to the use of visuals to engage the consumer's sight, and for some media, to sounds to engage hearing.

Since visuals are the predominant stimulus in most media, and since sight is the dominant human sense, efforts to attract attention must be designed to maximize the power of their visual stimuli.

Gestalt psychology provides the tools for such informed design through its insights into human perception. Gestalt psychologists study perception, and have established the insight that human perception is built around systems of pattern recognition which flow from the phenomenon of "emergence"; the human ability to recognize a whole that is more than the sum of its parts.

Pattern recognition is a "thinking fast/system 1" mental process. To conserve the cognitive power required for rapid mental processing, our brains develop short-cuts, which are formally known as "heuristics". Gestalt psychology identifies three core heuristics of perception.

The first is *reification*; our brain's ability to fill in aspects of a visual stimulus to create a whole. For example, it is easy for most people to quickly see a triangle (Figure 5.2(a)), and a sphere (Figure 5.2(b)), even though neither have been actually illustrated — only implied by what is there. This ability to perceive a whole that is greater than the parts is delivered thanks to a reification heuristic.

The second perceptual heuristic identified by Gestalt psychology is *multi-stability*; our brain's ability to see two patterns in one whole, and to alternate between them. The classic example here is Rubin's figure/vase illustration in Figure 5.3. Most people will be able to see two faces and a white vase, but they will not appear together. Despite intellectually knowing the figure contains both, understanding how, and even selecting which to see, when we do look, we're either seeing the faces, or we're seeing the vase.

The third core heuristic for pattern perception is *invariance*; our brain's ability to recognize the same

Figure 5.2
Reification

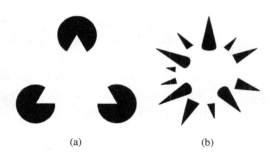

(a)   (b)

Figure 5.3
Multi-stability

object across many perceptual points of view, including their scale, rotation, and rendering. Steven Lehar has provided Figure 5.4, illustrating the invariance principle. We recognize that all the objects in cluster A are the same object, despite their different orientations, and we can easily contrast them to the objects in cluster B.

Everyone who has been asked to prove they are not a robot on a webpage will recognize the principle at work in cluster C of Figure 5.4. We can recognize the object again despite its distortion. And in cluster D, we still recognize the object despite the many different styles in which it is rendered.

The first key step in gaining attention is catching an observer's eye. Gestalt principles allow designers of images and scenes to maximize the potential that our brain's tendency to seek patterns will attract an observer's eye. The strong application of the foundational principles of reification, multi-stability, and invariance to images and scenes can be effective tools in attracting a viewer's eye through a reflexive and unconscious pattern-recognition impulse.

Figure 5.4
Invariance

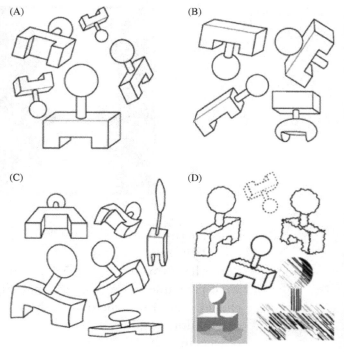

Gestalt psychology experimentation has shown that these core principles also combine and emerge as pattern structures. For example, the pattern-processing part of our brain seeks the ability to cleanly establish a center point around which an image or scene revolves. So providing *symmetry* in the design of visuals or video scenes may trigger a positive initial glance in its direction.

Our brains' pattern recognizing process is also drawn to *similarity* in visual design — our minds will work to create invisible (and conceptual) boundary lines around objects that appear similar to one another. This knowledge of how our brains will engage with content in the processing of patterns can also be used to trigger attention.

Content design for video, audio, and interactive formats should also consider how *sound and music* trigger attention. Capturing the consumer's ear can be as effective as capturing their eye. Volume is often used to trigger attention for advertising, but such attention might not always create positive association with what is being so loudly stated. Music is very much a pattern that can be shared through our design to trigger pattern response. Music delivers "hooks" that can trigger emotional engagement more rapidly than even visuals or a scripted narrative.

An impulse to find *closure* is another mental process that is triggered innately in our pattern recognition efforts, linked most strongly to the reification heuristic. Once our attention is engaged, our pattern recognition impulses seek to fit what we are seeing with our pre-existing understanding of the world. Thus, it may be possible to attract attention with a visual stimulus that does not immediately provide an explanation for its fit. We will look past those things in our environment that have a simple explanation for their being — including content that looks like all the other content we see in places where content is expected. But when content appears that does not provide easy closure, we may engage in an effort to achieve that closure. Headline writing — particularly the art of "click bait" — can achieve this for written words. Images and opening scenes that clearly show a dramatic beginning or end of an event will engage us to look into the story of what preceded or followed the image.

While all of the other perceptual heuristics defined here have potential to increase the appeal of content and thus success in getting people to look at our content, engaging the impulse to create closure once pattern recognition is triggered is the process that most effectively transitions our content from warranting a split second of attention to earning some concentration.

Filters: Consciousness and Concentration

Up to this point, our efforts to earn the attention of the content consumer through the understanding and application of Gestalt principles have been focused on sub-conscious and reflexive cognition. We've been dealing in split-second jumps of the eye, hoping that when that eye lands on our content — we've given it a reason to linger long enough to become mentally engaged. If that happens, we have arrived at the opportunity to move this engagement with the content consumer from sub-conscious to conscious cognition. This is a critical step in our effort to eventually drive behavior through our content.

The key distinction between consciousness and sub-consciousness is awareness. Sub-conscious processes happen without our awareness, while consciousness is defined by awareness. Awareness of something seems to require an entity that is aware, as one of the earliest philosophers of consciousness, John Locke, noted. This entity who has mental awareness is typically thought of as the "self". In this simple structure, consciousness then is when "I" (a self) think something and know that I am thinking it.

The philosopher René Descartes famously aligned thinking with being. With "I think therefore I am", he suggested that the awareness of thought proves the existence of a thinker.

In this logic, the "I am" observer is proven by the act of observation ("I think"), creating dualism between the thinker and the thought. It implies that a thinker is already there external to thoughts and is able to watch thoughts in the way a video is watched (in the "Cartesian Theater").

The critical factor in this premise — the thought itself — is conversely implied as a thing that appears before the observer — proving their existence through their ability to observe this thing. However, the notion of a thought that appears to be observed in one's head that is not first produced in one's head is a bit problematic under even the slightest consideration. Do we not produce the thoughts in our own head? If not, how do they appear from somewhere else? Can the act of thinking (consuming a thought) really be separate from (or come after) the act of producing a thought?

The Narrative Structure of Consciousness

A clean proposal for the answer to these questions about consciousness is proposed by Daniel Dennett in his book *Consciousness Explained*. Dennett proposes that consciousness is one of those "emergent" systems that matter so much to perception, with a sum that is greater than its parts. In Dennett's model, thoughts and a thinking "self" are actually co-occurring; the "self" that is thinking is produced with what emerges as thought.

In this notion, rather than a permanent core self that evaluates thoughts as they pass by (after emerging from somewhere else), our self is a constantly shifting, always emergent construct developing in tandem with our thoughts. Our sub-conscious cognition generates a constant and turbulent stream of mental impulses. When enough of those sub-conscious impulses begin to align, a "thought" (composed by a critical mass of similar impulses) emerges with a corresponding point of view ("self") to evaluate the impulses within the context of a narrative of past, present, and future. Just as DNA carries the core of a messenger RNA that then allows the DNA/RNA to shape a protein, so a thought (simply the potential to act/make/become) carries a self (thinker/evaluator) to determine what becomes of the thought.

In essence, our thoughts are signals built from collective impulses emerging from the noise, and our act of thinking is the act of fitting these thoughts into the understanding we have already developed of the world. Sometimes — hopefully as with this book — our thoughts don't fit what we already know and require us to find a way to expand our understanding of the world — to write new aspects into our story. But often — as proven by the predominance of heuristics in our cognition — we are able to quickly categorize thought and move on, following the script.

So, is there something to the idea that consciousness is really no more than being captured by a story we're telling ourselves? There's certainly always been some substantial thought given to the notion that the defining characteristic of our species is related to storytelling, and a narrative process of thinking that places us in that story.

Most people today will still sense the story that was being told in the ancient paintings on the walls of a cave. Our primitive ancestors who wrote this story would have lived their days within other narratives about the sources of light and darkness, of weather, of families and enemies, of what has been, what is, and what could come around the corner. We sense their story because in all the time between then and now, we can relate to the stories they lived. Because to be conscious is, and has always been, to be float-ing in a stream of thought about the past, the pre-sent, and the future related to concerns ranging from survival to success. And what is that stream of thought but a continually flowing story we tell ourselves?

Culture and Consciousness

Consciousness means simply that we recognize that we're thinking, and often also have awareness of what we're thinking about. When we're conscious of our thoughts, we also tend to be conscious of an entity of "self" or "I" — when we're conscious of thinking, we're also conscious of the thinker. But we often don't think of the nature of the self; our self is just there, in us, as something fundamental, core, and largely stable. We have history, a personality, and an identity, so we leave it at that.

Yet, when asked to stop and think, most of us would agree we're not the same person we were five years ago. Definitely not the same person as a decade ago.

And there are times when all of us think — or say — "that's not like me" or "I was not acting like myself". Could the self you were in those moments truly not be you? Did they somehow involve your physical self but not your mental self? What is the frame of time in which our self is constant? What is the frame of time over which it changes?

This all makes it seem that the "self" is more fluid than it is solid (which is lucky, or we'd have trouble learning and improving). In fact, the description we have of our self at any moment is itself one of our narratives; the one explaining how we got to that moment, who we are, and what we should do next. This narrative helps us know how to behave. Our "self" will prioritize thoughts that are aligned to a consistent (though not always constructive) narrative of self-interest. This individual prioritization of self-interest is the predominant target as a driver of behavior for those who sell and those who run for office, and we see it in action on sales floors on Black Friday and in the polls on election days.

The "self" that determines our conscious behavior is not a permanent "observer" sitting in the mind in a theater set apart from thought just watching what comes past, but is instead an emergent construct delivered with the mental impulses that have triggered our language and other sensory centers enough to warrant a "response" that positions these impulses in a narrative of past, present, and future, or cause and effect, which then indicates how we should react to them.

There are two questions inherent in this definition: (1) what shapes these mental impulses, and (2) what forms the narrative of past, present, and future or cause and effect that we use to evaluate these impulses?

"Culture" is the answer to both questions. From birth, the culture that surrounds us gives us our language and vocabulary, which in turn gives us the tools to order sensory impulses into concepts with meaning (good, bad, happy, sad, etc.), and thus the means to progress from utter helplessness in our environment and dependence on others for survival, to an ability to see, conceptualize, and leverage the structures of cause and effect relationships that help us avoid harm and accrue benefit. Over time, the mind releases impulses even without direct sensory stimuli, with memories of what's been experienced and concepts on what led to those experiences becoming abstracted into new immediate impulses without direct external cause.

What each of us manifests in terms of such abstract thought (i.e. thinking not in direct response to immediate stimuli) is a unique result of the combination of what we received as language tools, and the circumstances/environment in which we used them; or in other words, the culture in which we were raised.

All cultures contain the potential to produce the ability for abstract thought — though not all circumstances allow their application to the same challenges or opportunities. A child raised in poverty is as capable of developing brilliant thinking skills as is a child raised in wealth, though the opportunities to apply their brilliance is initially far more limited for a child raised in poverty than in wealth, as they have less access to the means that help apply their thinking to shaping their world.

In its first manifestation in our lives, culture is conveyed at the level of the family. What is enacted as culture in the family is often linked to the cultural norms of a close community, sometimes built around shared interests, sometimes forced by circumstances. Those community cultures are in turn shaped by larger cultural narratives (there's that word again) imparted through mediating structures.

American culture is built around concern for the self: self-interest, self-determination, self-identity. Democracy is premised on the notion that votes are made in one's self-interest or around self-identity, and that representation should be changeable if those interests are not met. Socialism aligns to a narrative of self-interest for people who cannot amass sufficient capital to meet their needs and believe they never will. Authoritarianism and totalitarianism offer narratives of self-interest to those who believe that the definition of laws and governance and justice and punishment are better placed in the hands of an all-powerful leader than in the hands of society at large. To want this, they must believe they would be protected under these laws (often while desiring that the competitors or enemies of their personal narrative would be punished), and would be left alone to pursue their economic self-interest while society was kept in a strict order that supported their personal interests. Capitalism is the economic narrative that most clearly aligns to personal narratives of self-interest and self-determination above all others, and can be woven equally well into either democratic or authoritarian narratives.

Cultural Mediation and Media

If the role of consciousness on politics seems like a strange place for this book to turn, please recognize that you picked up this book for guidance on how to use information to shape consumer behavior into conversions. The role of culture in shaping the thoughts that drive behavior cannot be separated from the role of thoughts and corresponding behaviors in shaping culture, and the behavioral locus for this interconnection tends to be in markets, and elections are a marketplace for ideas. The cultural narratives of a society shape who can become part of the political structure of a society, and how representative of the interests of society it will be. It is cultural narratives that determine what people think of as societal interests. (i.e. Which is valued more in the predominant cultural narratives, economics or ecology?) The political structure of a society is a cultural phenomenon that both reflects and shapes how people think. The political structure of a society shapes what can be sold, who can sell it, and what they can say and do in the act of selling. And the cultural narratives of a society shape how people think they should behave, including what they want to consume.

Whatever brought you to this book is what places you in this system — you are trying to shape what people want to consume. If you succeed, you will sell what you are selling, but you will also support or challenge cultural narratives located within economic and political narratives. This is your power and your responsibility when working to shape perceptions and drive behavior through media.

Concentration

Media as we think of it is the predominant mediating structure serving as a conduit for the thoughts that resided beyond us to come to reside within us. As articulated by Marshall McLuhan, media includes any such conduit. Human speech is the first purest form of media in this sense, imparting meaning and concepts that let us make (cause and effect) sense of the world.

From the narratives that were mediated through early utterances and cave paintings came new mediating structures including storytelling and drama, numeric systems and alphabets, mathematics, laws, religions and governments, painting, sculpture, architecture and engineering, schools, publishing, radio, film, television, chemistry, physics, information science, and digital media.

Each of these developments and branches in the mediation of thought share a common feature; they concentrate thought toward a distinctive result. In fact, many of the items in the list above can be found as "concentrations" in academic environments.

Turning back to the strict aim of this book and the arc of this chapter: our objective after gaining a consumer's initial attention through our intelligent use of design is to have them become conscious of our content; to have them concentrate enough on our content to pick up on our narrative.

This section's purpose is to establish the challenge that can be expected in earning conscious engagement with our content and turning initial perception to a moment of concentration — and thus the importance of designing content that increases those chances. Does your content appeal to the consumer's "self" within a narrative that will be immediately interpretable by them at the moment they concentrate on the message?

As you evaluate this, I encourage you to also consider how that narrative and the consumer's engagement with it influences culture and society. Advertisements and content products today are being assessed by consumers for the way in which they support or challenge cultural norms. At the time of writing, for example, the recognition of diversity in perceptions of the construct of relationships and marriage is in cultural debate, and advertisers who hope to be relevant by tapping into certain cultural narratives (such as what types of relationships to show in ads) will find themselves challenged for the side they seem to take.

There are plenty of examples of savvy content creators who understand how to tap notions of "self" and the cultural narratives surrounding them to drive results. Reinforcing people's preconceptions and fueling their fears and prejudices can lead to desired outcomes, It is hoped that readers of this book do not subscribe to "the ends justify the means" school of ethics, and that therefore tactics related to manipulation of harmful emotions will not be considered a tool for this book's readers.

By understanding narratives of "self" and self-interest, we can market an offering to fulfill a need or want. Content producers of every variety — from advertiser to publisher — should take responsibility for recognizing whether the fulfillment of the want or need is good for individuals independently and as a society. A lack of regulation against something that has potential or clear negative results does not make it right, and those of us working with data to convince consumers to consume should think about the rights and wrongs of consumption of specific types of offerings, and also of consumption in general. Consumption carries cost for the consumer, so we should have an ethical concern for the micro-economic impact of the conversions we are driving. Consumption (and the production that precedes it) uses natural resources and creates waste — so we should have an ethical concern for the environmental impact of the conversions we are driving. Physical consumption impacts the body — so we should have an ethical concern for the health impact of the conversions we are driving. Those of us working with data to drive consumption must be more than objectively neutral observers who simply point others to where the data says the most of a desired outcome can be generated. Evaluation is an aspect of analysis: and if we hope to maintain a consumer economy on a sustainable and collectively beneficial course, then we should accompany those insights with evaluation of the desired outcomes themselves and the consequences of fulfilling them.

If you are designing, producing, or distributing content, you share responsibility for shaping what we concentrate on as a culture and society.

Attention: Task-relevance and Task Distraction

Returning again to our tactical approach to engaging consumers with content; if we're designing content effectively, we've presented them with content that used design principles to garner their attention, and have incentivized them to concentrate with a narrative that engages them to interpret and place our message within their personal narrative.

Our final consideration on the attention side of our challenge to drive behavior relates back to all of the consumer research we've conducted before arriving at this point. The sense that consumers will have of our content's fit to their personal narratives will depend on how well we've understood one or more of the content consumers' Jobs to be Done (JTBD) in crafting our content.

As we consider JTBD fulfillment that will be engaged at this level of rapid System 1 cognition, we should consider jobs that serve a more foundational and less specified objective than we do when defining the JTBD of an actual consumer offering. The job that content does for a consumer to initially engage them to solicit consumption is less refined than the jobs that must be served once the full offering behind the content is consumed. But this does not mean the job is any simpler.

At the moment our content is encountered and presented as an option for consumption, it is very likely that our consumer is not looking specifically for our content. In the best case, our content will be presented as one of the results of a search, which means the consumer is already concentrated on finding something like what we offer, and our content's job is to convince them that ours is the best offering. We still need to give signals that our story will resonate within theirs, but we are at least doing so while the consumer's task at hand is related to the processing of narratives like ours. Such "task-relevance" of the stimuli being processed is an important contributor to attention.

As we move backwards from this ideal point of engagement, we find ourselves trying to have our content noticed at moments when the consumer's task is not explicitly related to processing content like ours. Beyond engaging them during a search, our next best opportunity to provide "task-relevant" stimuli is to align with the nature of what they are doing. If they are consuming entertainment through a video medium, then most likely the job they want fulfilled is entertainment, or possibly information. If we have designed our content for salience in visuals, sound, and narrative (i.e. legitimately humorous or ironically dramatic), we have a chance to be "task-relevant" in the consumer's interest to be entertained. The Superbowl is where the gold standard is set each year for video-format advertising content that is designed to entertain, but the effort to provide content that will seem relevant to the reason the consumer is consuming media is a full-time concern for advertisers, and for any other media product distributor who is trying to gain consumers' attention by inserting themselves in what the consumer has chosen to do.

If content is not capturing attention in a "task-relevant" way, it can be neutral and thus simply be completely ignored, or it can be "task-distracting" and thus capturing attention in a negative way. Neither of these alternatives to the consumers' sense of "task-relevance" for our content is desired, as neither is likely to help contribute to conversions.

The "task-relevance" of our content can be improved through consideration of the right contexts for our content and alignment of the substance of our content (design, copy/narrative, and sound as applicable) to those contexts. If we're offering a content product related to what they're doing (i.e. we're promoting a game within a gaming platform, or news within a feed, or videos on YouTube), then our content is well aligned to the task, and our challenge is primarily the successful capture of attention and the conveyance of relevance.

Advertisers have a more difficult challenge to appear task-relevant, as the content they're offering is meant to have consumers think about something other than their immediate interests at the time of consumption. Digital advertising platforms make it easy for anyone to drop their advertising into digital pages, social and video streams, but this approach gives little control (or thought) to how the advertisement will appear in context, especially when the driving factor for the advertiser is maximizing their dollar by making the least expensive placements. A well-developed media strategy will include consideration of "task-relevance" in aligning messages with media consumption contexts. Alignment of advertising content to the content being consumed through a website, magazine, podcast, or program provides the clearest "task-relevance", but also limits reach. Using digital signals about consumers' interests and behaviors, and being smart about the times of days and days of the week when consumers can be reached, opens up more opportunity to deliver content that may not be perfectly related to the reason for content consumption, but if it is noticed in the context of their consumption, will have a chance to register as relevant to that consumer.

5.2 Resonance: Building Memory

Sometimes attention and immediate concentration on a "call to action" is the primary goal in our conversion-driving efforts. When our content is the product, or when our offering can be quickly accessed through the same media as our content advertising (i.e. digital and e-commerce), then earning attention and concentration can drive consumers through a "call-to-action" that leads them into the process of conversion (i.e. subscribe, purchase, or download).

However, when our efforts are aimed at conversion that will occur at a time and place beyond the point of content consumption, and/or are aimed at brand associations and recurrent behaviors we hope to establish with consumers, then our content's mission is not to drive immediate and reflexive "direct response" conversion, but is instead oriented to a longer-term project of establishing associations, or put more simply: being remembered.

The objective here is to establish resonant associations between the brand and the consumer's context. Resonant associations mean that the brand is recalled as being "in tune" with the consumers' interests at a moment when a consumption choice is being made. In terms of the consumer journey, the resonance that an offering has established through content determines how highly the offering will be placed in the consumer's "consideration set".

Whether it be through education and "infotainment" that has been delivered to B2B buyers through branded content, or through an advertising program that has successfully built "mental availability" for the offering, or a series of video, audio, or headline teasers that have built anticipation of our content; for consumption that happens when the consumer is ready (versus right when they see our content), the objective is to establish our offering in their memory.

The content we're discussing in this book is not necessarily meant to teach in a literal sense (though news as a media product and B2B branded content certainly can do so), but it is meant to lead consumers to "learn" something about how our offering is positively associated with their narratives and needs. As with most memory structures, this "learning" can be established through strong emotional association, through repetition, or through a combination of both.

Emotional Encoding

Emotions deliver a strong connection between our physical and mental response to stimulus. From a survival standpoint, this linkage of the physical and the mental helps to create memories that shape and guide behavior from a young age, and through life. Stimuli that bring joy, establish trust, or offer surprise will become embedded with us as positive memories, and actions associated with these memories will be pursued and refined. Likewise, stimuli that create sadness, fear, anger, or disgust will become embedded with us as negative memories, and actions associated with these memories will be avoided.

Emotion has long been a tool applied to teaching. Unfortunately, a common manifestation is as negative reinforcement meant to develop submission to the authority of the teacher and the lesson at hand; typically brought about by creating fear or by cultivating anxiety through disapproval or contempt.

Better teaching uses positive emotions to build up memories that constitute learning. Establishing a feeling of trust, developing interest and anticipation, creating surprise and cultivating joy in the exploration of new things are all emotional attributes of a positive learning experience.

If our objective with content is to build memory structures that increase the chances of a consumer choosing our offering at a time that's right for them, then when we have a chance to reach them, our content efforts must help them learn how our offering is positively associated with their narratives and needs. Negative reinforcement is not a good look on any type of consumer offering, but positive reinforcement can strengthen the memory structures consumers have around our offerings. Content designers should consider the use of humor, suspense, and empathy to deliver feelings of trust, interest, anticipation, surprise, and happiness through the content, which will consequently strengthen consumers' positive associations with the brand.

It should go without saying, the quality and expected effectiveness of the humor, suspense, or empathy being conveyed should not be based on the tastes and takes of the creative team and managerial reviewers, but rather through testing among those we are trying to teach. Though most creative design is based on the premise that humor, suspense, or empathy are what makes creativity effective — they often resort to expert opinion in designing these versus a researched and data-driven basis for why the approach they've taken is the best solution for the audience being targeted.

Repetition

Repetition is a learning method familiar to anyone who ever studied for a spelling bee or worked with flashcards in their elementary school. Repetition is also fundamental to the established principles of advertising. Reach to consumers is understood by most advertisers to gain effectiveness through multiple exposures — but like many of the established principles of advertising — the reason why and how this is true is not often critically assessed. Returning to our collective experience with flashcards, it does seem like common sense — but a little more background can't hurt.

Research into advertising effectiveness over several decades has provided evidence to support the effectiveness of some repetition, and the "wear-out" or diminishing returns of too much repetition. A graph of message repetition effectiveness can be imagined as an inverted "U"; the impact of repetition climbs to a maximum point, then begins to diminish impact with further exposure.

The positive influence of the initially increasing exposures are explained by a rule of cognitive processing known as "positive habituation", which explains that new stimuli of any kind creates uncertainty, but that repeat processing of that stimuli reduces that uncertainty and increases receptivity. For repetition to allow content to reach that point of maximum impact, it must be coupled with a message that will actually resonate at the point that the consumers become receptive.

The declining effectiveness resulting from too much exposure results from cognitive tedium. Once the consumer has become habituated to the message, repeat exposures deliver what has become common, and increasingly boring. Over-repetition causes consumers to engage "slow" System 2 thinking around what they had previously understood through their "fast" System 1 processing as the task-relevance of the content, because the attention it draws now seems to distract rather than support the content consumer's pursuit of novel stimuli.

The topics of this chapter have addressed the core principles involved in the design of content intended to generate salience (attention) and resonance (from recall to engagement) with consumers. We have appealed to the senses using Gestalt principles. We have recognized the responsibility we have in shifting consumers' from perceptual sensation to concentration on a message. We have considered how we establish task-relevance once we have a consumer's attention. We have discussed the reflexive "direct response" behavior that can be prompted from that moment of attention. And we have discussed the longer-term objective of creating learned associations with our offering using tested emotional hooks and the right amount of repetition.

With all this in mind, the next three chapters turn to the tactics for developing and delivering experiences for content consumers through a wide variety of media with alignment to their consumer journey and consumer experience map.

Chapter SIX

To Mediate Should Mean to Motivate

Having developed content that we believe will earn attention and create resonance, we move from content design into the delivery of content through all the media falling under section "2. Interfaces and Experiences": including media networks and publishers, demand side platforms (DSPs), ad networks, social networks, digital platforms and application programming interfaces (APIs), email, experiential, and search (Figure 6.1). Whether an advertiser or media product offering — your content will reach consumers through one or more of these media.

Traditional advertising vehicles involve paid placement of video content on time-programmed television aka "linear" television (though now in streaming and on-demand video), as well as in print, radio, and out of home (OOH) content such as billboard and bus-stop sidings. These "mass reach" media are traditionally referred to as the "above the line" channels; a reference to accounting for advertising budgets that dates back to the 1950s.

Looking "below the line" we find reach through digital content in digital ad networks, social networks, digital platforms and through APIs. Direct marketing is delivered through CRM-based email and other

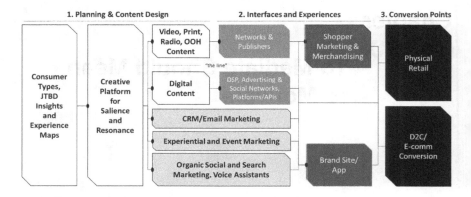

Figure 6.1
Interfaces and
Experiences

direct marketing (phone and mail). We also have search engine optimization (SEO) and search engine marketing (SEM) — the paid counterpart to SEO, both dedicated to ensuring the appearance of an appealing summary and link to an "owned" property of the brand for every search on a targeted keyword.

The process to get the brand's messages in front of an audience can vary from simple to extremely complex, but always requires some form of intermediation between the brand and their audience.

6.1 Media Strategy

This intermediation requires strategic planning. The ACAP introduced in this book is designed to support media strategy through its definition of the business problem and objectives, and the detailed insights about the consumers we are targeting, their Jobs to be Done (JTBD), and their consumer journeys and experience maps.

In addition to the understanding of both the business and consumer objectives and the results of research and analysis into consumer motivations and behaviors provided by the ACAP, media strategy will consider overall category performance and trends along with competitors' media presence. A media strategy will also further develop the consumer segment profiles with descriptions of their distinctive media consumption habits.

The media strategy should result in a high-level roadmap defining what types of content will be used to reach different consumers at different stages of the consumer journey. The following diagram (Figure 6.2) shows a very simple template for two age-based segments over three consumer journey stages.

Figure 6.2 Template for Two Age-Based Segments Over Three Consumer Journey Stages

This diagram uses ages for segments instead of the consumer profiles we developed for Icculus Industries only because of the intuitive sense this split on age offers around the expected applicability of certain technologies in reaching each group. An actual media strategy would replace these age segments with profiles like our Icculus Industries segments.

	AWARENESS STAGE		CONSIDERATION STAGE		CONVERSION STAGE	
	Media JTBD: Attention		Media JTBD: Concentration & Resonance		Media JTBD: Facilitate	
	18 - 30	30+	18 - 30	30+	18 - 30	30+
Linear TV						
Print Publications						
OOH						
Terrestrial Radio						
On-demand/ Streaming Video						
Online Audio						
Social Network Feeds						
Games						
AR/VR						
SEO/SEM						
Assistants						
CRM/Email						
Owned Web/App						
Online Shopping						
Shopper Marketing						
Live/Experiential						

The finalization of a media strategy would involve defining how each of these general media channels fits with a stage based on fit with JTBD (i.e. are search or virtual assistants applicable with generating attention), and fit with segment (i.e. while possibly good channels for generating attention, are terrestrial radio and print going to reach many people in the 18–30 category). Simply thinking through how and why each of these channels will serve as a good intermediary between our content and the target consumer for different stages in the path to purchase is a powerful strategic planning exercise.

6.2 Tactical Plan

At the end of strategic planning, the channels that will serve to intermediate between consumer's JTBD and our conversion-driving goals will be defined with a clear basis for each selection. From this, it is time to start selecting specific options for content delivery from within each of the selected channel categories above. This is the core of our "tactical plan", which will document our budget allocation and specific placement approach across and within each channel, and will also include a "flowchart" outlining when each type of media will be running over the course of a campaign or program (which could be set on quarterly or annual terms, for example).

The rest of this chapter and the next chapter will not focus on a specific recommended design for a media tactical plan, but will instead dive a bit deeper into the qualities related to reach, consideration, and conversion for each of the tactics that could be included in such a plan, working from top to bottom of the list in Figure 6.2.

Traditional Television

Traditional television is considered traditional in two ways: (1) it is delivered through a cable subscription (or in increasingly few cases via antenna), and (2) it is watched (often habitually) live or "time shifted" but still in the same day (i.e. recorded on a DVD), which is common for gameshows, news, and sports.

Traditional television serves programming from broadcast networks (like NBC or CBS) and cable networks (like Food Network or the USA Network).

Television is a powerful reach tool based on the size of audiences that can be targeted, but also based on the multi-sensory and immersive nature of the medium. With well-designed content, television advertising can earn attention and concentration, but the consumer's "task" while watching television is typically not directly conversion related, so the "task-relevant" objective of television beyond creating attention should be about developing awareness and associations, without the expectation of driving immediate conversions.

Other "Above the Line" Tactics

"Above the Line" tactics can be thought of as synonymous with "mass marketing" tactics, which aside from television include linear radio (stations with time-based programming), print, and OOH media like billboards and transit coverage. These are primarily consumed when the consumer's task is something other than conversion-oriented, so they should be used for attention and awareness/learning.

From a gestalt standpoint in earning attention, *radio* offers the most immersive option among these through its ability to combine music or sound effects and narrative. However, the reach of linear radio is time constrained (often around commute) and demographically constrained as well — your reach will be smaller, and competition for the best opportunities will be higher. If radio can capture attention, radio is a good medium for establishing "learning" around the brand — but beware the "wear-out" factor if that lesson is repeated with too high a frequency.

Print can provide a very "task-relevant" and contextual vehicle to earn attention for content, as most magazines are topical, and you can very likely find topics that match the JTBD behind your content. Delivery through print requires lead-time, and the more the topic is focused, the lower the likely reach behind each placement. Magazine advertising does have the potential to build positive associations with the brand, as the medium itself and the design of print content can convey a "premium" aspect to the topic of the content.

OOH media like billboards and transit placements (i.e. bus stops, subway platforms, and train car placements) offer large reach opportunities — lots of people will be exposed, and they will be exposed day after day as they go about their routines. However, OOH media is challenged on the attention-earning front. There may be some interactive options as with digital bus-stop sidings, but for the most part, the message is limited in copy and visuals. And the message will be competing with other billboards, sidings, and posters, all trying to be noticed in consumer contexts that are dedicated to moving from one place to another and not to digesting content. In some cases, as when people are commuting on mass transit, mobile and app-based calls to action could contextually make sense. Unfortunately, while mass-transit content can easily present a call to action ("call us", "download now"), the limited nature of the message may also limit the ability for the content to actually justify and motivate the desired action. Thus, the primary objective for OOH should be attention and brand awareness.

Digital Video

As we move below the line that separates traditional mass media from more targeted activity, the media options present the opportunity for the development of awareness and attention, as well as interactive engagement to help drive concentration and consideration.

Our first stop "below the line" is in digital streaming for video and audio. At the time of publication, streaming video is available in several varieties (and there may be more by the time you read this). Like traditional television, these video formats have the benefit of multi-sensory and immersive engagement of attention, with strong potential for awareness and concentration when the content is done well. Unlike linear television, these formats have the additional benefit of specifically defined targeting, and so can be shown only to households that have exhibited a high likelihood of interest in the JTBD we are offering to solve.

A large swath of what is delivered through digital cable has developed into *Addressable TV*. Addressable TV carries broadcast and cable network programming that is consumed like linear TV, but the digital format allows cable providers to target advertising content to specific household characteristics including demographics, purchase behaviors, viewing behaviors, and online habits, all of which are often conducted through an internet pipe provided by the same cable company that is helping advertisers target their ads.

Cord-cutting — the separation of video viewers from cable contracts — has introduced more options for video consumption, including video on demand (VOD), often served over the top (OTT) of a cable provider.

VOD is served through subscription platforms like Netflix, Showtime on Demand, or HBO Now, through "TV anywhere" platforms like Hulu and Sling, and from channels or apps from broadcast and cable networks and other content producers (like Crackle or Newsy). It is also available from free platforms like YouTube, and increasingly as an option from cable providers. With VOD, consumers can browse and watch any programming available through the platform at any time, and through any device. All video that bypasses a cable box and streams through an internet connection instead is known as "OTT" content. Watching OTT on a television requires an internet-connected TV, or a device like Apple TV, Google Chromecast, Roku, Amazon Fire, or a gaming console. VOD can be accessed OTT on other devices directly through apps belonging to subscription and free platforms.

Subscription OTT has no advertising, but all other OTT does deliver advertising that can be targeted, like addressable TV, to household characteristics including demographics, purchase behaviors, viewing behaviors, and online habits.

Finally, digital streaming also includes audio streaming through internet radio and music platforms as well as podcasts. Like terrestrial radio, advertising within online music and podcast content is a good medium for potentially establishing associations around the brand. Unlike terrestrial radio, digital audio can be more effectively targeted, and exposure can be better controlled to avoid the "wear-out" factor that comes from too much repetition.

Digital Publications and Networks

The most basic form of digital targeting is conducted like print targeting, through placement in publications that have readers that match the characteristics of our target consumer. This approach can be implemented through direct placements with publishers or through selection of publication topics and audiences established by the advertising networks and exchanges.

Google Ads is the tool for Google's *advertising exchange,* which sells the inventory for Google's search and display *ad networks.* Google's is not the only network of advertising inventory across digital environments — there are many. Neither is Google the only ad exchange. But Google does offer a comprehensive, simple, and accessible option for display targeting, we will begin with a specific look at delivering ad content through this tool. Google's options represent the standard digital targeting capabilities available through all exchanges, so the understanding of what is offered here represents the fundamentals of developing reach through digital publications and ad networks.

Delivery through Google Ads is built around a "campaign". When setting up a new campaign, the platform's set-up assistant interface will ask for an objective (which this book's readers will have defined through the ACAP). At publication, the objectives that can be selected are sales, leads, web traffic, product and brand consideration, brand awareness and reach, app promotion or none.

Depending on the objective selected, Google's UI will suggest types of campaigns. *Standard display* can be used to reach out to "look-alike" audiences from existing lists of customers or for "re-marketing" to those who have engaged with your digital properties before. Standard display can also be set-up to target specific demographics or audiences that have been built by Google around consumers' interests and habits and their current online behavior indicating a life event or purchase consideration. *Shopping ads* allow merchants to promote their products with photos or video and dynamically generated headlines, prices, and availability details. These ads use geographic and "in-market" targeting variables to expose ads to online targets with what the algorithm believes is the highest propensity to buy. *Video* ads use similar targeting variables — demographics, interest, and behaviors — and the ad engine wraps the video with headlines, a call-to-action, and an end-screen to encourage interaction.

Programmatic Digital

The most advanced option offered by Google Ads are "smart display" ads, which combine several programmatic targeting approaches. Programmatic simply means that a software program — an algorithm — is dynamically adjusting details about the targeting. These adjustments are made to optimize spending, the reach to targets that will respond to advertising, and the content of the ad that drives the best response.

Spending optimization is conducted through real-time bidding (RTB), which optimizes the efficiency or cost/benefit ratio around qualified impressions by considering the expected value of each impression, and determining how much to therefore bid to have the chance to present content to that impression.

The real-time bid involves a micro-second negotiation between what the publishers or their representative network proposes an impression is worth to interested bidders, and the value that all advertising bidders are willing to place on that impression. In this exchange, each side is calculating a value of the impression, and will have a limit (bottom for seller and top for each buyer) they want to achieve in the exchange. Thus, the determination of what to pay for an impression must be based on a clear understanding of the expected value of that impression. Ad network reporting on performance should be expected to deliver insights into not just how they managed cost, but how they also maximized expected value per impression for that cost.

Optimizing reach and response requires an ability to present the content that is expected to perform best wherever the highest propensity consumers are found across the digital environment. Dynamic ad building works with components including headlines, videos, and images and descriptions and assembles them to work in any ad format (from large screen to mobile, and video players to text search).

Optimizing value requires the programmatic algorithm to seek the most responsive audiences for the content. This algorithm is continually looking for the consumer characteristics most strongly correlated with conversion and targeting people with those characteristics. This may mean that the consumer characteristics that are being targeted change over time from what was initially set.

Paid Social Media

From a user standpoint, social networks are applications that serve them a curated and highly relevant and engaging content feed. From an advertising or content publishing standpoint, social networks are another digital network used for targeting content to consumers.

The purpose and approach to paid social marketing is similar to that of all other paid media marketing, with the key distinction being the direct interactions with content that show social networks what consumers are interested in, and with whom they share those interests.

Most social networks offer their own exchanges for developing audiences, setting objectives, managing delivery, and measuring results. Facebook's exchange, for example, offers placements across Facebook and Instagram as well as in sites that serve ads for Facebook.

In social networks, targeting is built around age, gender, and location. Targeting can be refined around life events, financial status, relationship status, interests, and behaviors. On social networks, an understanding of interests and behaviors is directly measurable: from explicit expressions of status and interest in the "about me" sections, to interactions and engagement with content within the network.

Social networks are interactive by design — so content delivered through social media should be designed with the intent to capture attention and drive engagement through relevance to the audience. The format should be designed with specific consideration of the nature of the network and the audience; for example, what works on Facebook may not work on Twitter, though Facebook content may be reusable on Instagram.

Demand-side Platforms, Data Management Platforms, and Customer Data Platforms

To round-out this introduction to targeted paid digital communications, we should take a quick side trip to review three Ad Tech/Mar Tech tools that facilitate digital targeting and, in some cases, link it with owned channel targeting: the demand-side platform (DSP), the data management platform (DMP), and the customer data platform (CDP).

DSPs allow advertisers (those on the demand side of the advertising transaction) to manage their content delivery across multiple advertising networks through a single interface. Without a DSP, advertisers would need to search inventory or set targeting rules, buy impressions, and track performance through multiple interfaces with the variety of ad networks they are utilizing. The DSP allows coordination of paid advertising through a single interface.

Coordinating that advertising around standardized target audiences often requires the addition of a *DMP*. DMPs integrate and standardize data from first and third party data sources across paid earned and owned media around a shared unique identifier (UID), allowing advertisers to develop audiences that are consistent and applicable across all channels. DMPs will contain some tools to allow for data mining and statistical analysis of this integrated data, and can make this data accessible to any other tool that the advertiser chooses to use to conduct such modeling. They also allow for audiences developed through such modeling to be communicated back out to the networks and supporting tools (DSP) through which these audiences are accessed.

Oracle's DMP BlueKai offers web users the ability to see what a DMP knows about them by visiting the Oracle Data Cloud Registry web page (active as of publication). The registry exposes the way the DMP sees the web visitor — which determines whether the user would be offered up for RTB based on the targeting criteria of an ad.

The categories exposed through the DMP are similar to those that Google Ads exchange uses for targeting (Figure 6.3).

Figure 6.3
DMP
Categories

Within each of the categories above will reside anywhere from one to hundreds of pieces of information. For example, according to this website, the "Hobbies & Interests" category for me contains 240 targeting criteria.

DMPs expand advertisers' ability to develop and target audiences from anonymized behavioral and transactional data that extends well beyond what is available through a single exchange. The activation of these audiences against more than one exchange would be facilitated through a DSP.

Targeting through DSPs and DMPs is conducted around anonymized UIDs. Each user we reach has a persistent unique ID tracked through these systems, but the specific identity of each individual and their personal information (like contact information) is not available. This allows DMPs to develop groups of people into "audiences" based on all available data for targeting, but limits the actual delivery of content only to those sources that can match the UID to a piece of identifying information (like which specific browser or device is theirs). Thus, while it may seem that an advertiser "knows" what you browsed when you were last on their site even though you never gave them personal information because you see it again in ads across the web, the advertiser doesn't know anything about you specifically. They've simply used their DMP to place your anonymized UID into an audience of prior browsers and tasked their DSP to show content related to that visit whenever they find that anonymous UID again on the web. They're not showing ads to what you think of as your identity, but they are showing ads to an anonymous entity that they do know has been to their site and viewed some specific content.

If one of those ads worked and brought you back to their site, and if you then shared information with the advertiser to create an account or place an order — at that point, you would move from being just an anonymous UID to becoming a de-anonymized "user" of their system. This transaction would create records in two places; a CDP and a customer relationship management platform (CRM). CRM and its partner marketing automation (MA) systems are oriented around transactions, and so will be discussed further below.

CDPs create records of any digital interaction with a consumer — so are like DMPs with the ability to track specific users. CDP records can be linked back to DMP UIDs, so we can place specific customers and our knowledge of how they've engaged with us back into anonymized (but highly personalized) digital targeting audiences. Once a CDP has tagged a person with their own UID, they can link what that consumer does within owned properties (behavior on website and apps) with shared property engagement (authenticated social engagement with the brand) and tie that back to targetable dimensions through paid channels via the linkage of the CDP

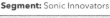

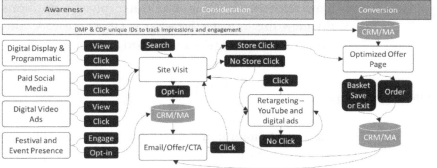

Figure 6.4 | UID and the DMP UID held in the DMP (paid
Consumer | targeting dimensions can never be imported to a
Experience | de-anonymized record).
Mapping |

Returning to the Consumer Experience Map introduced in Chapter 2, an important element of the
map should now make more sense. Across the top of
the map, under both "Awareness" and "Consideration",
there is a call-out: "DMP and CDP UIDs to track
impressions and engagement" (Figure 6.4).

All of the consumer's movement through the paid
and owned awareness and consideration channels
would be completely disconnected without that common thread of behavioral tracking offered by the
DMP (which traces a persistent anonymous ID) and
the CDP (which allows us to track against specific
identities).

CRM, MA, and Email Marketing

The diagram above shows a line running from
DMP and CDP tracking through CRM and MA to an

"optimized offer page". The "CRM/MA" database icon also shows up in two other pivotal positions through the journey. So what is CRM and MA, and what part do they play in the consumer journey?

CRM and MA

CRM tools maintain records for existing and prospective customers. Every customer or prospective customer has a record indicating whether they've purchased before, what they purchased and when, and where they are in the cycle to purchase again. Prospective customers are also tracked and evaluated for whether and when they are expected to purchase. CRM systems also maintain records of customer's other interactions with the brand, including calls to a call center, email communications, or requests for servicing or support. In the diagram above, CRM records are created when consumers provide their email and opt-in for subsequent communications with the brand. CRM is also accessed when a site visitor reaches the store; either accessing their existing profile from a logged-in state to learn what might be offered, or creating a record when a new log-in is registered to allow a basket save or purchase. And finally, whether they save something to their basket, exit without action, or make a purchase, their CRM record will be updated with what that means for their place in the purchase cycle.

In our experience map, each of these CRM updates has an associated follow-up action in the MA system. An MA system can be a simple automation tool, automatically executing some pre-determined follow-up to a step in the consumer journey that might have been executed without software, but which can now be scaled and delivered more immediately and responsively through software-driven rules. However, MA systems can apply predictive analytics to decisions around whether and when to next engage a consumer after the trigger of a previous journey step, and even what content should be used from among multiple options as the best choice for driving consumers through the journey.

In the map above, the person with a new CRM record created by opt-in from our event marketing then receives an email through our MA system. Those consumers who reach the store have a customized page served to them with elements defined through what our MA system predicts will most likely cause conversion. The MA system will trigger re-engagement of consumers who reach the site and enter content in their basket but don't buy with email or retargeted advertisements. And consumers who buy will be sent a different email on different timing to encourage their next purchase.

While different MA platforms have some differences in their design and user interface, the underlying approach to dynamic delivery through these tools remains largely the same:

1. Use dynamic content delivery capabilities to "personalize" engagement, dynamically delivering push-messages (email, mobile/text, and ads) optimized for the best probable response for each user.
2. Suppressing or escalating certain forms of engagement, and dynamically selecting the best content for each interaction.

3. Continually evaluating the "lift" in probability to convert created by sequences of channel and content interaction for users of different types over time, and update probabilities for propensity scoring and delivery optimization scoring accordingly.

This last step, evaluation of incremental lift by channel (and ideally the specific content within that channel) across the entire "path" constituting the customer decision journey, and the assignment or "attribution" of credit for a conversion to each channel, has been a well-established topic of analysis outside of MA for some time in the form of attribution, which will be discussed further in Chapter 8.

Email Strategy

As just discussed in the MA section, email marketing is a popular and common tactic used for direct contact with leads.

Since email systems existed even before web browsers, email marketing was also the earliest form of digital marketing. Early email "targeting" tended to involve selection based simply on the fact that the recipient had an email account. As email accounts became increasingly common, and browsers allowed websites to send people to see, email marketing proliferated so quickly and so broadly that email inboxes had to be fit with "spam" filters and junk mailboxes to deal with the influx of marketing efforts through email.

Of course, unsolicited junk mail through an inbox does not meet the relevance criteria discussed in this book, and is usually as appreciated as an unsolicited sales call in the middle of dinner. But the practice of email marketing is cheap and easy. So despite the fact that if an unwanted email is acknowledged at all, it is more likely to alienate the receiver than it is to persuade the receiver to take the desired action, mass emailing is still a foundation of many marketing efforts.

Through a "task-distraction" effect, email marketing can quickly become a waste of time and budget if the strategy behind it is not built around delivering relevance in context. But with the right strategy, it can also be a very effective part of an integrated marketing program. Effective email marketing focuses first on maintaining a good list of targets, meaning we are only going to email people for whom (1) email is an effective channel for engagement, and (2) an email from us will have relevance to them (if presented correctly). These two rules mean that email through our CRM system to users who have opted-in are good, while unsolicited emails to purchased emails lists will have a low success rate, and may backfire by generating negative attention.

Recognizing that email is usually only welcome in specific contexts, email strategies should set realistic expectations around the results they can expect. With this in mind, email strategy should be designed to work in concert with marketing engagement through other channels, and should include email marketing as a part of their orchestrated, multichannel marketing plans designed for customer decision journeys. MA software can facilitate this orchestration.

Mobile Games, Augmented Reality, and Virtual Reality

Efforts to gain consumers' attention must always be careful not to impose themselves where they are task-distracting. While mobile advertising through apps offers the opportunity to deliver targeted impressions, it also runs a significant risk that this content will interrupt the consumer's intended task.

Mobile advertising — including mobile reach through the display and social networks described above as well as through game-based advertising — allows targeting for location in addition to the demographic, attitudinal/interest, and behavioral targeting that all digital ads can utilize. For advertisers with physical locations, this location-based targeting ability can help focus content on consumer's who are (or have a history of being) in proximity to a physical location to encourage their visit.

Advertising through *mobile games* is most commonly delivered through impressions purchased from an existing game as a third party, but the cost/benefit option to directly create and launch an "advergame" can be considered by some advertisers as well — especially those who already offer content as a product. Content delivered through a third party has higher potential to interrupt the desired experience (playing the game itself), while a branded "advergame" can create highly active engagement for the presumably short period that the game remains novel to players.

Advertisers can access in-game advertising through specialized mobile gaming exchange partners. Mobile ad views are encouraged by the game-developers through explicit inclusion of rewards for completing ad views as an aspect of the game experience. While players must pause their actual gameplay as it is interrupted by an ad, the in-game reward for the ad view may "gamify" the ad experience enough to avoid the negative consequences of "task distraction".

Advertisers seeking to deliver their own branded mobile game experience might look to an established platform as a base. For example, the Facebook Ad Exchange (delivering through the Facebook platform and their broader "partner sites" network) offers a format called "Playable Ads" which delivers interactive video that delivers a game experience without requiring an app download. As with all other formats, good gestalt-based thinking in content design is required to earn attention and concentration.

Augmented reality (AR) content offers the potential for high attention and engagement with content for a brief time, but may have high barriers to earning initial impressions. AR simply involved overlaying digital content on a physical environment. This is most frequently accomplished through the use of a phone's camera — though wearables built for AR like the somewhat infamous "Google Glass" have emerged in beta and will likely become more widely adopted in the years following this edition's publication.

Although it still sounds futuristic to many people, at the time of this edition's publication, AR is already widely utilized in several forms, with Instagram filters and the game Pokemon Go chief among them. While apps and games allow users to easily discover and use AR filters, AR as a vehicle for earning attention to advertising content requires instruction and set-up that makes it better suited to in-person introduction than simply media-based adoption. And *Virtual reality* (VR), which requires a special headset and earphones or earbuds to be worn in order to place the user completely into an audio-visual environment, requires the same direct engagement with consumers. For this reason, AR and VR today are perhaps better tools that assist in live and experiential marketing than they are independent marketing channels — but that will likely change with time.

Experiential Marketing

Experiential and event-based marketing delivers direct engagement between a brand and consumers in a physical environment. This can range from having a few product spokespeople giving away free drinks in a popular bar to an after-hours special event at a flagship store to a large sponsored installation at a multi-day festival that treats people to free giveaways, experiences, and services.

Experiential and event marketing are intended to deliver branded experiences that create awareness of the brand and ideally generate affinity for the brand. Experiential and event marketing should enhance the time the consumer is already having in their physical environment, so efforts to drive conversion will typically not be appreciated unless consumers came to the experience or event with an intention to convert (i.e. a food festival or craft fair, or an event held in a flagship store or other retail environment).

While experiential marketing will not typically aim to drive conversion, it can pursue lead-generation objectives along with its primary objectives to build awareness and affinity. For example, at the largest annual motorcycle rally (490,000 attendees in 2019), which takes place in Sturgis South Dakota, Progressive Insurance hosts a large installation called "Flo's Chop Shop". Named after their "Flo" spokescharacter, the installation is a salon for bikers — offering haircuts and beard trims, hair braiding, manicures, and even boot polishing — all free. In exchange, Progressive has the opportunity to create a relationship with each participant. Each participant is also invited — unobtrusively at some point in the experience — to sign-up for further contact from Progressive. No motorcycle policies are expected to be sold from inside Flo's Chop Shop, but strong "mental availability" can be created, which brings the brand into consideration when policy renewal time rolls around. If the consumer has provided their contact details — they may receive a few reminders before then as well.

As mentioned above, AR and VR can be compelling elements of experiential or event marketing. For example, Icculus Industries could establish booths at summer street festivals where visitors are invited to use their phones to virtually design their ideal guitar using a custom AR filter, then to take and share a picture of themselves as rock gods. This interaction could also create the opportunity to follow Icculus Industries on social media, or ask for opt-in to further communications. Icculus Industries could also offer a custom VR experience in this booth — letting people wear VR goggles and headphones that place them on the stage of a sold-out stadium concert and lets them rock through an opening song. For many people, the novelty of this addition to their experience of the event would justify the requirement to sign-up with an email to get their turn.

Content Marketing and Branded Content

Content marketing seeks to develop affinity for the brand (and resulting positive mental availability) by providing useful or interesting free content. Content marketing is a popular method for establishing and maintaining business to business (B2B) marketing relationships, and is also popular to maintain relationships used around non-profit memberships and other donations (e.g. alumni associations) as well as high consideration consumer purchases (like health-care, eyewear, games and electronics, or musical instruments). Delivery of content as a whitepaper or case-study, infographic, podcast, blog, video, or news-letter are some of the most common options. As with event marketing, this tactic is not expected to directly drive sales — it is meant to establish a positive connection between consumer and brand. However, branded content will often be offered with a requirement to enter contact information in order to access the content. This may limit the reach that the content achieves to reach its primary objective (building affinity) in exchange for a focus on leads.

Once consumers exchange something valuable for the content (their email) — it is no longer entirely free — and therefore will be held to a higher standard in terms of the value it provides in return. Consumers are wary of click-bait in any guise. A marketer who require a lead for their content run the risk of establishing negative mental availability if the content received in exchange is not perceived to have been worth the sharing of information, especially once that information turns into follow-up emails or calls. There is very little point putting time and effort into content marketing that will alienate the target consumer, so the quality of the content product is critical in content marketing. This is why marketers who are committed to content marketing as a tool for developing and maintaining affinity and mental availability will build a team of professional content production staff including trained journalists, editors, and designers. The provision of personal information to professionally produced trade publications, specialty magazines, podcasts, videos, and websites will feel like a subscription to any other valued content source.

Branded content is a derivative of content marketing that is not an advertisement with a call to action, but which includes the brand in content meant to inform or entertain. This content can be provided for free, or sold as a media product. The LEGO toy company, for example, has a YouTube channel with over eight million subscribers and 10 billion views of content. The site offers build challenges, designer insights, LEGO stop motion animation, and product spotlights. LEGO has also produced a series of movies, animated programs, and video games as paid content, which the YouTube channel also features with movie and game promotions.

Chapter
SEVEN

Content and Experience Makes or Breaks Conversion

Chapter 6 introduced the many media that are available in the effort to reach consumers and try and earn their attention and even concentration. In Figure 7.1, these fell under section "2. Interfaces and Experiences" both above the line in video, print, radio, and out of home (OOH), and below the line through digital content, customer relationship management (CRM), and experiential and event marketing. This chapter shifts our focus further "below the line" into paid and organic search, owned websites and apps, shopper marketing, and direct-to-consumer and e-commerce sales.

What differentiates these tactics and channels is the fact that consumers must "opt-in" or proactively engage with these media to consume your content. This means that they have determined that your content has some degree of task-relevance for them. With search and voice assistants, consumers are expressing their interest, and ideally finding your content as a match. And with organic social media, they find the content compelling enough to pass along (increasing its reach).

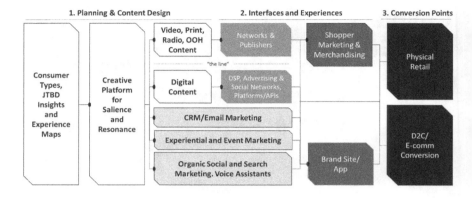

Figure 7.1
Interfaces and
Experiences

7.1 Search Engine Optimization, Search Engine Marketing, and Organic Social Media

Search Engine Optimization

Search engine optimization (SEO) emerged in the early days of digital marketing as a specialization focused on understanding the inner workings of search engines' content ranking algorithms and applying that understanding to drive their site to the top of search results. As the sophistication of search algorithm's increased, the ranking methods of the algorithms shifted to a focus on the quality of certain types of content related across sources versus the simple presence of certain content (e.g. the site description tag) or the quantity of certain types of data (e.g. backlinks), and the opportunities for "gaming" these algorithms began to diminish, separating true SEO specialists from simple rule exploiters.

With contemporary search engines, SEO is not a simple matter of tweaking portions of pages and building volumes of links, but is instead completely inter-related to site design and content strategy. Search engines look deep into websites, not just to assign relevant keywords with that site but also to evaluate and rank the quality and relevance of the site's content against those keywords. With the increasing utilization of dynamic page content, the impact of site design on search presentation is an important consideration from the beginning of the design process. Additionally, the correct set-up and maintenance of meta-data within the content management systems which will populate sites becomes a critical effort for search engine optimization. Thus, the SEO manager of today is less a simple editor of links and tags, and more a manager of quality assurance around the myriad aspects of site design, development, and content that determine the site's appearance in search results.

The first concern in SEO is information about keywords. How will a search engine view your site in terms of the keywords it finds within the content? Conversely, what are the keywords driving traffic around your key topic among your targeted audiences? Analysis of these two areas will reveal the core challenge of the SEO manager — matching up what can be found on the site with what people are searching for.

Understanding competitive keywords can be easily accomplished through many tools, but is free through Google Ad Words as long as you have set up an account. The "Tools" section of Google Ad Words offers a "Keyword Planner" which allows for keyword identification for any page. These results also provide listings of the competition per keyword and suggested bids, which indicate the value in terms of relevance to searchers for those terms. The return on investment (ROI) of SEO can actually be determined by evaluating how much was saved on winning traffic on these terms organically versus via purchased search results.

Appearing at the top of a competitive search is not just a game of simple presence or quantity of target key words. With text-analytics software being used in indexing algorithms, the name of the game now is quality and relevance in the content of your site, and clarity in the way it is presented. One way in which Google suggests SEO managers convey the relevance of their content is through links from high-quality related sources. Google is now smart enough to know if links to your site are coming from "link farms" which exist solely for the purpose of creating links to try and fool search engines. There is no quick way to create high value links, as Google notes, "Google interprets a link from page A to page B as a vote by page A for page B. Votes cast by pages that are themselves 'important' weigh more heavily and help to make other pages 'important'".

As further proof of the fact that SEO managers need to be involved in the design and mechanics of the entire site, note the technical aspects of the design relayed in Google's statement above that need to be evaluated if the page is not conveying content to search engines as desired. Before they can begin to solve problems with search optimization, SEO managers must be able to identify and frame problems for the developers who will ultimately help them solve those problems.

Search Engine Marketing

Paid search, or search engine marketing (SEM), is the paid counterpart to SEO, dedicated to ensuring the appearance of an appealing summary and link to an "owned" property of the brand for every search on a targeted keyword. SEM placements against keywords are purchased directly from search engines.

Like SEO, SEM delivers content that is triggered by clear user intent — a search on a related term. SEM is not "earned" media. Content matching to keywords and the impressions that are served against that match have been paid for. Search engines do however require that the content being served is relevant to the keywords. A content server can attempt to purchase (bid on) any keyword they desire. However, the search engine algorithm will review the content of the site, and if the site's content is not task-relevant to the search, there's no way that site will win the bid. Search engines rely on relevance and credibility of results, so it is not in the interest of search engines to "bait and switch" consumers from a search on a topic to a site that has nothing to do with their interest.

SEM is targetable like other paid media; the engine can be told to bid only on consumers with specific characteristics or in specific contexts. This benefits the search engines, the consumer, and the marketer, as it increases the probability that content will be served to someone with a higher interest in converting to the ultimate goal of the search.

Organic Social Media

Fundamentally, what makes social media effective is the value of the content in driving a social exchange. Users of social media networks create and post content not just to share, but to hopefully earn a response to what they are sharing. People use social media to exchange communication with others.

In organic social media marketing, reach is accomplished entirely through consumers' willingness to engage with and share content. Each time a qualified prospective or existing customer engages with us or talks about us or shares our content for others to see, we are meeting the core objective of organic social media: being social. We are generating a valuable and credible type of awareness through peer referral, and we are potentially creating affinity and deepening loyalty through our interactions. What we are not doing however is controlling who receives our content — that is a matter of self-selected engagement driving impressions to their network connections. And there is no promise that those network connections will be the consumers we would have selected if using targeting options, or that they will find our content relevant.

If we've approached the design of our social media strategy with a conversion science mindset, then every interaction and impression creates another kind of value; learning about customers and prospects. An understanding of who we're communicating with is the most critical foundation for communicating effectively.

7.2 Voice Activated/Digital Assistants

Voice activated search is a natural evolution in the use of mobile digital devices. Voice search can be conducted through phones or interactive peripherals such as (at publication) Google Home Hub or Home Mini, Amazon Echo, and Apple HomePod.

Voice search on Android phones and Google Hub or Mini is conducted through the Google Assistant application, while Apple phones and the HomePod use the Siri application. The Amazon Echo peripheral runs the Alexa app.

Google's Assistant is integrated with the Google ecosystem and Apple's Siri uses Google search by default, while Amazon's Alexa uses Microsoft's Bing search engine but is directly integrated with the Amazon e-commerce platform for shopping-related search.

Creating web-based content that is optimized to appear in the result for a voice search requires an evolution of SEO-based thinking in digital content design. Site content will need to be optimized for full questions like "who are the best custom guitar designers?" Responses should be short to encourage the search assistant to index this result for voice response. On a technical front, page speed is also a significant driver in being indexed for voice response.

While questions are one form of speech that voice assistants can address to surface your content, the response to commands is another digital assistant function to potentially leverage.

Commands function through apps that the assistant has been told to apply by the user. A "play music" command will open the user's defined music app with instructions from the assistant on what to play. "Turn on the front room lights" will open the user's connected home app for lighting with instructions from the assistant on what lights to turn on. "Add paper towels to my shopping cart" in Alexa will default to the Amazon market and in Google will engage the Google Shopping network.

Steering conversion into your service through commands to digital assistants requires having the user define your app as the preferred channel for completing an action, and establishing the connection between the assistant and your app. For example, Icculus Industries could develop an app that offers personalized reviews and recommendations with an online shopping option. The download of this app could be promoted through a related voice search response. Once the app is connected to the digital assistant (through the Google Actions or Alexa Skills application programming interfaces, for example), it can be made the default to answer musical supply related questions, or to respond to commands like "order new guitar strings and picks". If an order has been placed before, the app can be trained to make a purchase based on items in prior orders. If the order has not been placed before, the assistant may offer options and ask for a selection.

Voice search and commands are at the extreme end of "task-relevance". Not only is the consumer's intent very clear through their search, but the voice format engages the consumer with minimum effort. This is why voice-enabled interaction with consumers will continue to grow as the front-end of digital UX.

7.3 Web User Interface and User Experience Design

Consumers' visits to websites are typically highly "task-relevant," in that they are only accessed through intentional effort, which means the people who arrive have decided to be there. With a website, the challenge is to make visitors stay, then engage in a desired action — which can include opting in to further communications, finding a location, subscribing to content, or making a purchase online.

The first requirement for any landing page (where visitors arrive from media or search results) is that it is optimized for every screen size, from the very large to the very small, and that it should load very quickly. Assuming that basic design concern is covered, the next step in getting users to stay and engage is all about design (gestalt again) and content.

In terms of design, the user interface (UI) should provide the simplest possible approach to the most possible requirements of a visitor. Color, font, and images should be used to draw consumers attention to what they are expected to find important. That most important content should be in the most prominent position on the page, and the hierarchy of content should be clear using position, headers, font size, color, and spacing. Other content within the site but not on the first page should be easily and clearly identifiable through simple and concise navigation menus. In short, good UI delivers a site that allows visitors to simply, productively, and enjoyably engage with the content of a website.

A site's user experience (UX) includes the quality of interaction with the site as mediated by the UI, but it also includes the content that is accessed through that interaction. UX design defines what is expected to be the most important content for visitors, and the hierarchy that resides beneath that. UX design anticipates visitor's motivations and goals, and ensures that the experience delivered by the site fulfills those. Therefore, UX designers should be connected closely with consumer insights research and analysis. And UX and UI designers will directly conduct interface design-focused research and testing of various UI options.

UX designers will be the primary users of web and app metrics covering everything from bounce rate for visitors to the page (indicating how well the page establishes value on first impression) to what is being viewed, to how visitors are searching, navigating, and exiting the site. And of course, measurement will establish how many visits result in the targeted conversion objective — be it opting-in to further communications, finding a location, subscribing to content, or making a purchase online, depending on the nature of the site. And analytics will help establish how these results are segmented by various factors, including visitor characteristics, traffic sources, times of day and days of week, and the way people moved through the site or app to arrive at the desired conversion (or not).

Web Design Blind Spots and Dark Patterns

Organizations are smart to pursue UX designs that maximize conversion — but only as long as they do so with value to the consumer in mind. In some cases, the desire to raise conversion numbers can lead to UX design that loses sight of consumer interest. These designs are so focused on the business' interest, they are prone to "blind spots" in terms of whether they are actually helping the consumer. If conversions are being earned by deception — even unintentionally — they are likely doing more long-term harm than good.

A few years ago, I worked with a client who sold a high-consideration product offline through large retail chains, and used digital marketing in search, web, social media, and email to guide comparison shoppers through product feature descriptions and value propositions over a multi-touch decision journey in the online environment.

Because this client was not able to track users from the site to the store to truly understand how digital marketing efforts contributed to sales, their executive team had decided to evaluate the value of digital (and the performance of the VP of Marketing in delivering that value) in terms of a "proxy" measure for sales, which they determined should be a click on the "where to buy" (WTB) call to action for each product on the assumption that at least some of these would actually convert to sales.

Under pressure to deliver what executives considered to be "conversions", the digital marketing team was asked to find ways to increase "WTB" conversions. In evaluating opportunities to drive up this KPI, one digital strategist noted that the Canadian version of the site had a higher WTB rate than the US site. On investigation, it turned out that the Canadian site did not show pricing on the product detail page as did the US site, but instead showed pricing only on the page served from the WTB click.

Seeing this as the basis for the higher rate of WTB clicks on the Canadian site, the US team decided to test a change to their site that would match the Canadian site, moving pricing off of the detail page and behind the WTB click.

As a result, WTB clicks on the US site did increase. Luckily, this client allowed our analytics team to accompany this test with a satisfaction survey. Although the key performance indicators (KPI) were improved, the survey showed that satisfaction with the site was much lower in the test version than in the control, and many comments suggested that the frustration caused by having to look for pricing had soured them on the idea of selecting this brand's product. While the test had achieved a result in increasing a marketing KPI, it had actually done so by decreasing clarity and increasing friction, and the result of this degraded UX was an overall decrease in the value of the site to users and the business, despite the increase in the marketing KPI. Needless to say, we advised the VP of Marketing not to implement the "winning" result, and began to help the organization rethink how they measured the value and success of their digital marketing.

The case above illustrates the unintentional sacrificing of good UX in exchange for a business outcome in an approach that I call a "blind spot" because the organization has become blinded to the bigger picture in focused pursuit of a marketing KPI. However, there are many unfortunate cases when the sacrifice of UX from manipulation of that experience in pursuit of a marketing goal is not unintentional, but is in fact quite intentional. The creation of such intentional manipulations of experience in pursuit of a KPI have become known as "dark patterns".

Dark Patterns are intentional experience design "patterns" driven by the desire to maximize short-term outcomes without concern for the longer-term consequences. Thankfully for web users everywhere, since 2010, a group of UX professionals has been focused on documenting these deceptive marketing practices whenever they are found via their website "darkpatterns.org". This group of UX designers has identified 14 dark patterns that companies engage in to intentionally deceive users in pursuit of higher performance in certain KPIs. While pursuit of higher performance in marketing is the objective, if the proposed design appears to align with any of the dark patterns below, readers of this book should know to raise their concern over the use of a strategy that uses deception to increase a KPI.

Following are definitions for a few of the more relevant patterns of concern from the "darkpatterns. org" website:

- **Bait and Switch:** "The user sets out to do one thing, but a different, undesirable thing happens instead. This is one of the oldest tricks in the book, and it is very broad in nature — many dark patterns involve some kind of bait and switch".
- **Disguised Ads:** "Adverts that are disguised as other kinds of content or navigation, in order to get users to click on them".
- **Forced Continuity:** "The user signs up for a free trial on a website, and in doing so they are required to enter their credit card details. When the trial comes to an end, they automatically start getting billed for the paid service. The user is not given an adequate reminder, nor are they given an easy and rapid way of canceling the automatic renewal. Sometimes this is combined with the

Sneak into Basket dark pattern. This dark pattern was previously known as 'Silent Credit Card Roll-over,' but was renamed since the term 'forced continuity' is already popularly used in Marketing".

- **Hidden Costs:** "A hidden cost occurs when a user gets to the last step of the checkout process, only to discover some unexpected charges have appeared, e.g. delivery charges, tax, etc."
- **Roach Motel:** "The 'Roach Motel' is a broad category of Dark Pattern that subsumes most types listed on this site. Put simply, a Roach Motel makes it very easy for a user to get into a certain situation, but then makes it hard for them to get out of it when they realize it is undesirable. Email newsletter un-subscription is a well-known example — whereby it is typically easy to subscribe, but much more effort is needed to unsubscribe. The revised CAN-SPAM 2008 rules state that this practice is forbidden for emails that have a primary purpose 'to advertise or promote a commercial product or service'. (Unfortunately, CAN-SPAM does not cover 'transactional or relationship' messages.)"
- **Sneak in Basket:** "The user attempts to purchase a specific item. However, somewhere in the purchasing journey the site sneaks an additional item into their basket, often through the use of an opt-out radio button or checkbox on a prior page".
- **Trick Questions:** "The user is required to respond to a question (typically in the checkout process), which, when glanced upon quickly appears to ask one thing, but if read carefully, asks another thing entirely. This pattern works because it is normal for users to employ high-speed scan-reading on the web".

7.4 Applications

The careful reader will have noticed an occasional reference to "apps" in the website section above. This is because the principles of UI and UX design that shape effective websites also shape effective apps.

Apps are software residing on the user's device that perform some task for the user. Apps are often best utilized with a connection to the internet, but apps do not need a connection to the internet for at least some of their functionality to operate, and some — like games — may serve their purpose even when no network connection is available.

The conversion objective for many app makers is to have their app installed and used. For these content producers, awareness and consideration of apps is generated primarily through targeted paid media and search within app stores. The value they gain from conversion can come through a fee charged for the app, or from the monetization of users through in-app advertising.

Aside from serving content and UX as a product, other types of apps will provide content and UXs that facilitate interactions and transactions with brands. For example, payment apps can facilitate transactions at bricks-and-mortar points of sale, and banking apps can allow users to manage finances from anywhere. Apps facilitate ordering food or groceries for delivery, ordering a car, a train ticket, a plane ticket, or a hotel, finding a date, and of course, shopping for anything and having it shipped to your home. Mobile apps have profoundly changed where, when, and how brands can transact with consumers.

7.5 Shopper Marketing

Despite the convenience with which most things can be bought online, people still spend time in stores for a variety of reasons. They may just need something right away, or they may find browsing physical items to be the best approach to evaluating their options and deciding. They may have seen something they like online, but want to experience the product in real life before making a purchase.

Once a consumer is in a store, the planned efforts to convert them are known as *shopper marketing*. Shopper marketing uses cues in the consumer's physical space to encourage purchase. These can range from the lighting, layout, and music in a higher-end retail space, to physical displays and free samples at the grocery store.

Shopper marketing is becoming more sophisticated through the use of in-store digital and planned engagement with mobile. When shoppers have a retailer app installed on their phone, the phone's GPS can be used to identify when that person is in a physical location. Digital apps can send alerts with items of interest or special offers and can encourage consumers to scan items while in-store to search for instant rebates or to add to a wish-list. Digital apps can also use store mapping to help consumers plot the best route through the store to pick up everything on their shopping list.

Augmented reality (AR) is an option for engaging consumers through their digital devices. In store signage can prompt consumers to scan these signs for more information on the product's details, colors, and sizes in stock, and even customer reviews. Large screens in-store can offer AR filters as "virtual mirrors", allowing consumers to virtually "try on" products without changing clothes. Some products will encourage consumers to scan their packaging to see the labels become animated. And customizable products can use AR to let consumers "design" or customize the product they're seeing in-store.

Digital shopper marketing culminates with an ability to reduce friction in making purchases. The use of "tap and go" digital wallets facilitates payment for people accustomed to shopping with their phones. And online retailer Amazon is in the lead with efforts to pioneer the next generation of automated checkout, using sensors and computer vision through their Amazon Go stores to allow shoppers to simply pick items off the shelves and leave, with their payment being taken automatically from the Amazon Go app. This digitally enabled seamless retail may have become even more common by the time you read this book.

7.6 E-Commerce

As we've reviewed digital marketing and communications capabilities above, many of them have had their ultimate terminus in an e-commerce transaction. All of the digital media and apps we've discussed have offered the potential to drive consumers into an online purchase interface. Media as a product from news to entertainment to games or apps are often accessed through online purchase as a subscription or download. It is the goal of most direct digital media to lead consumers to conversion in a digital environment where the conversion can be tracked, or to a physical location with links to digital media as discussed above.

E-commerce is quite simple in concept: items for purchase, descriptions, pricing, delivery information, and customer reviews are made available to shoppers. Shoppers have a "shopping cart" where they can queue what they want to buy immediately, and a "wish list" where they can store items they are considering for later purchase. Purchase from the shopping cart is made as seamless as possible; first-time shoppers are given the easiest path to completing their purchase, and repeat shoppers have the option to store information to make purchase possible with a single click.

As with any sort of commerce, the challenge in e-commerce comes from getting prospective customers into the e-commerce environment, and then motivating them to purchase. The customer acquisition challenge has been addressed throughout the preceding pages. Increasing consumers' motivation to purchase once they are on the site requires the combination of data and design.

Recall that under the conversion section of our experience map, all of the information we had about an individual visitor as captured through their anonymous behavior (DMP) and their identifiable behavior (CDP) was passed through our CRM to link it with their past purchases and their estimated current readiness to purchase. This profile was then used to trigger site optimization through our marketing automation tool.

That optimization would take place on the visitor's landing page. Our system's knowledge of what that visitor has been shown, what they have engaged, what they've done previously on the site, and where and when they've purchased from us before all shape what will be shown on the landing page for that visitor. Predictive dynamic page optimization will determine the hierarchy of what is shown on the landing page, and will decide how to include offers and incentives, as well as the calls to action intended to prompt entry to the purchase flow. Whether selling content as a product or products promoted through content, the final step before online conversion is an experience with point-of-sale digital content that should be optimized to drive the transaction.

Chapter EIGHT
It's Never Good Enough

With choices made from among the vast array of touchpoints we can utilize to engage consumers on their journey from awareness through conversion, and with our objectives and experience designs developed through the first two sections of the ACAP, let's turn now to the more engineering focused aspects of conversion science.

8.1 ACAP Section Three: Testing

The strategic and design processes behind digital content and user experience often reach a point in their process where a decision about the "best" approach is required. While this decision can sometimes be effectively made based on professional experience, prior data, and a knowledge of best practices, there are also frequent cases when none of these can be applied to the question at hand, either because there are multiple and differing opinions around what experience, data, and best practice suggest would be the best course, or because none of these are applicable to a new content or experience design challenge we are trying to solve. In these cases, rather than guessing, the smart marketer will turn to testing or experimentation to develop a data-driven position on how to proceed.

Every marketing approach we want to recommend, and the competing approaches our colleagues might recommend, should all be understood as a "hypothesis" about how the work we do will cause the outcomes we desire.

When we are not willing to stake a definitive claim about what causes the outcomes we are seeking and hold that claim up to scrutiny, but instead want to generate insights by trying several different things and comparing their results, we are conducting experimentation.

The major distinction between experimentation and testing is in the nature of the hypothesis and what it requires from a design standpoint. With experimentation, our hypothesis is simply that there will be some identifiable difference across variants once we observe the different approaches in action, though at the outset we aren't sure where or why those differences exist. The number of variants we evaluate is limited only by available samples and acceptable levels of cost and risk. We need a correctly sized sample for each variant, and the more variants we experiment with, the harder it gets to find enough samples. And of course, each variant we develop and run as an experiment carries cost and a risk that it may not perform above average in terms of results.

With testing, our hypothesis always defines some specific cause that we expect will produce an above average effect. This specificity in the definition of cause and effect means that the number of variants will be limited by the number of specific causes we can reasonably defend as potentially driving above average outcomes for a group of people. Thus, testing against clearly defined hypotheses will be less costly and time consuming in terms of developing samples, and will carry less risk than experimentation since we'll have designed a test variant on an informed basis for expecting better performance.

Testing can be done within paid, owned, or earned media through two approaches: A/B/n testing or Multivariate testing (MVT). A/B/n testing is the more straightforward of the two approaches. In this approach, a "control" version "A" is tested against a change in one variable through one or more test versions (designated "B" through "n"). In MVT, there are multiple test versions, each of which contain some unique combination of several variables being tested. MVT is beneficial when there is a hypothesis that proposes that a change of several variables will result in a better outcome than a change in any one variable, and allows the conversion scientist to run a single test to understand the lift provided by each possible combination of changed variables as opposed to needing to run a sequence of A/B tests for the same understanding. The challenge with MVT testing is in the rapid growth of versions as variables are added, and the size of sample therefore needed to reach statistical significance in the results. In a simple A/B/C website test, traffic to the element being tested is split 33% each between the three versions, which means that we can quickly collect a large enough sample of visitors in each case to make the results statistically valid. In an MVT test of three variables however, there would need to be 27 versions to test all possible combinations of all three variables, meaning each version gets less than 4% of total traffic. With such small numbers coming to each version, the time it will take to reach statistical significance for each version will be quite long.

Designing a Test

Given the sample population required for the simple A/B test defined above, the sampling challenges and design complications inherent in MVT testing should be clear. Accordingly, we will focus on the A/B approach to testing for the remainder of this chapter, though it should be relatively obvious how most of these principles can apply to MVT testing as well.

The first step to testing is to define and document the goal you are seeking from the test. Test goals are most commonly related to improving performance around a key performance indicator (KPI), such as increased click-through in digital advertising, or increased engagement with a web page's primary call to action. The goal may be defined in terms of a specifically quantified increase, but typically goals are simply targeted against a "significant lift", the higher the better.

With the target KPI defined, the next step is to identify one variable that we think could be changed to create significant improvement to our target KPI, and to explain, in the form of a hypothesis, why that change will produce improvement. Often, organizations will reach this step and realize they cannot actually explain *why* they think a change might produce results, and are simply seeking to see if the alternative they have would work better than the existing approach. In this case, the test is actually an experiment. Running experiments to better understand how marketing works is not a bad idea, so there is no problem with this approach as long as it is acknowledged explicitly, and is not an experiment masquerading as a test and trying to hide the lack of a hypothesis.

Whether we are running a test with a hypothesis, or conducting observation through an experiment, in an A/B approach, our objective is to see a lift in outcomes by the alteration of a single variable. In a test, the justification for the variable we chose and the change we make to that variable are defined in our hypothesis. The variable we chose may be related to any number of elements in the digital experience, it may be the location of an ad, image, or text, it may be the content of the ad or copy of the text, it may be the structure of a form, the sequence in which content is presented, or the way in which navigation is structured. In all of these cases, our basis for improving performance of the experience will typically be related to resolving an experience barrier or improving an experience driver. Below are several of the most common drivers/barriers:

- **Clarity:** A lack of clarity in the reason for or purpose of a message or experience is a sure barrier to performance, just as increased clarity can be a driver of improvement in performance. You don't want content viewers or site visitors to be confused by or lost in the experience you deliver, and if there's a chance that they are, then increasing clarity at that point is a good testing focus.
- **Consistency:** A close cousin of clarity, a lack of consistency throughout the experience a user has

in digital channels can create a sense of incongruity, and drive people away from the experience before they reach the point of conversion. A common area of missed consistency is in display advertising that drives users to a landing experience that does not align with what was communicated in the ad. Content, copy, and user experience (UX) that does not maintain logical consistency throughout the site or across channels (e.g. being unable to find something on mobile that was easy to find in a laptop browser) can also generate a negative response. Failing to "remember" details about a user within a site experience as moving from page to page or section to section (e.g. what was provided in one form is asked for again on a subsequent page) is a major failure in consistency, especially as users expect sites to remember them (with their permission) from visit to visit.

- **Value/Urgency:** In display advertising, on the website, in email, and even occasionally in social media, at some point in the digital experience the visitor should feel compelled to act. A digital experience that fails to convey a sense of value or urgency somewhere within its most engaged elements is clearly not working hard enough to drive users to a conversion. An effort to more effectively convey value and/or urgency is perhaps the most common basis for testing, and rightly so. If the path to conversion is indeed being presented clearly and consistently, but users still aren't converting, the next clear area of focus is in ensuring that there is effective communication around the value or urgency that users should feel in following that path.

- **Friction:** A well-designed and/or well-tested experience will present users with a clear and consistent experience that guides them toward a compelling presentation of value and/or urgency to act. The next barrier to conversion is friction in the process required to complete the conversion. This is most commonly related to content input required by users, for example, forms with too many fields or too many options in several look-up fields, or forms that are not designed well for input on mobile platforms. Technical issues, such as pages that are slow to save or slow to load, can also cause friction. Forms that can be started but not saved, requiring re-entry on a subsequent visit, violate good experience in terms of both consistency and friction.

- **Anxiety:** A close cousin of friction, anxiety causing elements include a lack of clarity in the reason for the collection of information, or requests for certain forms of personally identifying information (PII) such as social security number. While personalization and consistency are typically desired by users, there are times when the insertion of personal information or a sense of over-familiarity within digital communication (especially off-site display re-targeting) can seem "creepy" and create anxiety.

While our focus in A/B testing should be on transforming just one variable, the transformation may address more than one of the drivers/barriers defined above. In a test, improvement in at least one of these areas should be the basis of the hypothesis.

Context, Context, Context

In creating and evaluating the results of a test, it is not only the hypothesis of the test that matters, but also the way in which it is designed, conducted, and evaluated. The importance of sample size has been discussed already regarding research. Another consideration around the sample to ensure statistical significance is the requirement that the sample is truly random, in that it proportionately represents participation by every type of person (segment) you might engage in the experience being tested beyond the test environment.

Once the test has collected enough samples to reach statistical significance, the conversion scientist should explain the outcome as clearly as possible. If the test version showed lift, the analyst will restate the hypothesis in explaining the result. If the test version did not produce a significant lift, there will be no explanation for the failure to achieve this result in the test data itself. In such cases, the reason for the failure to produce an outcome is that the hypothesis was incorrect, or more pointedly, the basis for the hypothesis was incorrect. The results of a failed test do not contain clues as to what to do differently in the next test, they only contain clear guidance on what would not work if tested again.

One valid "dig" area in the evaluation of test results is in outcomes against segments. As stated above, the attitudes and characteristics of different groups may cause them to respond differently from the average response. Isolating responses from specific segments and evaluating results for these segments against the entire sample may reveal that what did not work for the entire population does in fact seem to work for a small portion of the population. With the capability for dynamic targeting inherent in digital marketing, such knowledge can be very beneficial; though we may not push the tested approach to production at large, we can use targeting to serve the tested approach to members of the segment that respond better to the tested version than to the control version.

Testing Across Channels

Marketing's purpose is to create an impact on consumers to increase their propensity to buy the offering being advertised. Testing channels allows us to evaluate the variety of ways in which this can be accomplished. In general, our objectives will involve understanding, for a specific audience or audiences, whether and how much:

- *Having a campaign* works better than no campaign.
- One *creative* approach works better than others.
- Certain *combinations of tactics* produce different outcomes.
- Different *frequencies of exposure* produce different outcomes.
- Different *sequences of exposure* to creative produce different outcomes.

Testing across marketing channels is done to collect data about one of the questions above that we did not previously have. In doing this, we may need to challenge some of our tendencies to use the data we have to optimize around our existing understanding of what works best.

Interestingly, programmatic targeting is built precisely to take randomization out of media delivery. Programmatic targeting optimizes what is served against a target outcome. If a common characteristic of people who trigger our conversion tag is that they over-index in purchases of natural products, then our engine will begin serving the same ad to everyone with an above average purchase pattern for natural products. The problem here is that while interest in natural products and conversion to our product may be correlated — there is no evidence that exposure to the ad we're serving in any way caused the purchases. In fact, what could be happening is that we're just steering ads toward people who would have bought anyway without them. Ironically, this will still show a positive Return on Ad Spend (ROAS) since the people who are shown the ads also buy, but it does not prove that showing the ad is what made people buy.

ROAS is a ratio metric, not a volume metric. So ROAS-oriented clients may be okay with programmatic limiting of their reach to "look-alikes" as long as they see a high rate of conversion. However, really effective targeting and ad serving reaches people who are not likely to buy without some prompt and gives them that prompt. For every person who is motivated to buy via this prompt (and wouldn't have bought without it), the advertising has delivered incremental sales. This is not to say the advertising will be the only part of a marketing mix that drove the sale, but it is a contributor in the mix.

Testing is required to prove that advertising is actually causing lift versus simply inserting itself into sales that would have happened without it. And conducting this testing will require that the group of people who don't see the ads are statistically equivalent to those who do, meaning testing must be conducted without programmatic optimization in place.

This may concern clients who have been trained to see ROAS as their ultimate measure.

In testing what makes people convert, we can test within the same demographic, psychographic, and behavioral segments we're targeting against, EXCEPT for segmenting on a proclivity to convert — which is programmatic's main determinant. The proclivity is the variable we want to be truly randomized. When clients are used to targeting based on seeking the highest conversion proclivity, they will need guidance and discussion around a core concept required to support testing: that for a test, reaching more people and seeing some of them fail to convert may be more valuable in the long run than reaching only those who look like people who have already converted. It may be more valuable because the audiences who don't look like prior converters are where the biggest opportunities for growth from new consumers reside if their interest can be unlocked.

As we test into these audiences, we know that at first we will see lower conversion than we would with targeting narrowed around look-alike models. But as we continue to test and learn with these audiences, we have the potential to find what does work to raise conversion among these audiences, and to differentiate those by how much they work for each audience, thus growing the overall volume of consumers for whom our targeting can be effective.

8.2 ACAP Section Three: Performance Measurement

We turn now to the nitty-gritty aspect of marketing; the evaluation of its performance against goals.

Most of our discussion up to this point has related to how the mechanics of communication to drive conversion works, what platforms we have to communicate through, and what methods we can use to design an approach to engaging with consumers that best serves our chances of earning a conversion. Experimentation as discussed above is an effort to try multiple approaches to achieving performance and learning from the results. And testing as discussed above is a more methodological assessment of various options that we have a basis for thinking should improve our results. Dynamic, algorithmically-guided optimization of content delivered, and even user interfaces, through the orchestration of DMP, CDP, and Marketing Automation is intended to increase the performance of our communications throughout the consumer's journey. The big question for business-minded managers in all these cases is: "is it working?" Performance measurement gives us the answer.

Paid Media

There are several different KPIs that are commonly used to measure paid media performance. Each measure reflects a variation in approach that is typically driven by strategy, objectives, and the data used to support these.

Impressions/Gross Rating Points/Target Rating Points/ Cost per Mille and Cost per Point

The way in which an advertiser engages with advertising networks and exchanges is directly related to how they work with data in determining their strategy and measuring their performance. If an advertiser's strategy does not include a measurable conversion as a core basis for determining "value", then it is likely that the objectives will fall to lowering the cost as much as possible for the greatest corresponding number of impressions.

Impressions are the result of our communications' reach multiplied by frequency of exposure. Reach tells us how many households or individuals were exposed to our content. Each individual or household is counted only once. Frequency is the number of times that each of those households or individuals will be exposed to a message.

Gross rating points (GRPs) are an "above the line" metric most commonly used for TV that contextualize impressions as a percentage of the population. Target rating points (TRPs) are the same measure, but with the population narrowed to only those who are our targets.

The basic efficiency performance KPIs around impressions are CPM, which stands for "cost per mille" (cost per thousand impressions), or cost per point (CPP). Being rooted in impressions, or views, these "cost-per" measurements (and any strategy based around them) are still removed from any concerns for what actually results from an impression of an advertisement. Cost-per measures take the delivery of impressions as an end result, as opposed to the means to an end. Of course, marketing outputs are not the same as business outcomes, so marketing strategies based on impressions and "cost-per", while they may be focused on optimizing spend against impressions, cannot claim to be focused on optimizing any sort of business outcome, as there is no basis in this measurement to evaluate whether the marketing output (a cost) actually led to a business outcome (a return).

Brand Awareness and Perception

Having read this far, you know that the path to conversion begins with attention and awareness, and that these ideally build to positive perception or "mental availability". Awareness of the brand and related perceptions can be measured through brand tracking surveys. These surveys ask consumers to identify the brands they associate with a category without prompting (unaided awareness), and also list brands and ask which ones the respondent knows (aided awareness). They can ask whether the respondent has seen advertising for a number of brands. They will ask respondents to select their opinion of brands from high to low. They may offer specific messaging or positioning, and ask which brand is associated with that message.

Measuring awareness and perception as a result of marketing provides better insight on the impact of marketing than does simply measuring reach and frequency. To do this, the results of each brand tracking instance must be evaluated against prior performance, and the context around each point of measurement. How did consumers answer these questions when the survey was run six months ago? What did our advertising look like then versus now?

Improvement over time is good to see, and the context around what might be driving that improvement is important to assess. However, improved brand awareness and perception are not business results. Awareness and positive perception are critical means to drive a desired end in conversion. Measuring these as "ends-in-themselves" objectives of marketing means that marketing is disconnected from the organization's conversion mission.

Click-through Rate/View-through Rate/Cost per Click

Measuring impressions, costs-per, and survey-based awareness and perception as performance KPIs are generally the only options for traditional print, television, and radio touchpoints, as there is no way to effectively measure the response to those impressions. However, the capability to measure engagement with content and consumer journeys through digital channels allows for much better measures of performance for digital advertising. Thus, advancing slightly from measurement of CPM are the measures of click-through rate and view-through rate (CTR/VTR) and cost per click (CPC).

The "click" referred to in these metrics is any interaction with links in digital content. CTR is a ratio of actions per total impressions, and as a measure of engagement — while it still does not measure an actual business outcome — it is at least capable of measuring the response to content, and as such conveys data that can drive further optimization of effectiveness in creative content and channel placements.

VTR is a variation of CTR which has become increasingly used as a metric for measuring not just the immediate reaction to an advertisement via a click, but also the potential for delayed reaction for an exposure to an advertisement. VTR measurement uses a tag to recognize when a visitor to a site arriving through any referring source has been exposed to paid content, and counts that exposure against the visit to the target destination, meaning that even though the visitor did not click-through the content (assuming they could), the visitor has nonetheless come through to the destination at some point after being served (and presumably viewing) the ad. VTR thus allocates credit for the visit back to the exposure to the content. While this method likely includes actual cases where the cause for a visit is a delayed reaction to an advertising exposure, it likely also gives credit for visits to ad exposures that were not the cause for an eventual visit (i.e. the ad was served to a person who intended to visit anyway), or were much less effective than a subsequent brand exposure through another channel like social media or email. Approaches to "attribution" as a method to properly assign some "partial" credit to every touch-point that contributes to a visit are discussed further in what follows.

CPC is a measure of the efficiency of the CTR achieved. If optimizing to CTR, then CPC will rise and fall according to the cost of reaching the size and composition of audience that maximizes CTR. If optimizing the CPC, then CTR will be affected if the ability to reach an audience that is more qualified to click is limited by a ceiling on the cost of reaching that audience. Thus there are serious budgetary and strategic concerns to balance when holding an interest in cost with an interest in outcomes.

Owned Channel Metrics

Web, mobile, and email analytics platforms and the marketing automation (MA) tools provide comprehensive analytics reporting and dashboards for an understanding of channel performance, and most also offer the capability to develop good context around that performance and draw insights for research from the data.

Email metrics tend to be very functionally focused around the key metrics of delete rate, open rate, un-subscription rate, and click-through rate. Beyond these, email is measured as a referral to other channels within those channel's dashboards versus within an email report. So while we can see the open rate and click-through rate in our email metrics, our insight into what happened after that click-through will come from metrics in the channel that received the referral — which is typically a web landing page — as long as we tagged the click to pass along the right information into the receiving channel. Thus, the descriptive analytics in an email platform are typically used to evaluate the response of different segments of recipients to all of the content that has been sent to them, including to evaluate the results of content tests within a segment (e.g. testing the response to two different subject lines, or calls to action).

Most web and mobile dashboards provide some predefined views organized around types of visitors, sources of traffic, and the classic stages of the consumer funnel through which they pass in their consumer journey.

Acquisition metrics deepen our understanding of the sources of traffic to our website or app. These metrics may feed performance measurement against acquisition objectives set for traffic-driving channels like organic and paid search, email, social media, and display advertising, but it should be remembered that acquisition (e.g. "click-through") is not an end in itself, it is simply an initial means to the end we desire for each visitor, conversion into our defined macro conversion. As measures of performance, acquisitions metrics are the basis for setting and measuring channel performance optimization against conversion goals. Acquisition metrics also provide useful context to aid this optimization such as comparative campaign and keyword performance.

Audience metrics exist to provide context around the types of visitors, augmenting performance metrics and supporting research in descriptive analytics, and are critical to the segmentation and targeting efforts that are central to prescriptive and predictive analytics. Audience metrics typically begin with straightforward demographic metrics of age, gender, and geography, and technographic variables around browsers and devices used to access the site. All of Google Analytics' audience metrics are built from what they know about site visitors based on the Google advertising cookies each of those visitors carries in their browser, and many other platforms also incorporate or can at least integrate with data from advertising cookies from multiple sources. When this link exists, audience data also includes summaries of the interests and market segments of site visitors, which can be used to develop segmentation, guide content creation, and target the delivery of that content.

Behavior metrics will typically provide measures of marketing KPIs, and provide critical context around user's interactions with the site, revealing patterns over time around behaviors leading up to conversion or non-conversion. These metrics largely fall into the "context" and "research" sections of the analytics pyramid, and are critical in allowing us to develop insights into what works, what doesn't, and form hypotheses around what might work better.

Behaviors that we measure on the site include pages viewed as the most basic measure, and the visitors' interaction with pages as measured through the events we might have established, site search, and the paths users take through the site.

Entry and exit pages are the most basic metrics of interest around pathing. Entry pages are typically driven by our acquisition efforts, while exit pages are based on alignment of the experience to the users' needs. "Bounce Rate" is a commonly evaluated metric related to exit pages, measuring the cases where the exit page is the same as the entry page, and thus measuring the effectiveness of landing page content in encouraging deeper interaction with the site among the audience coming to that page.

The importance of considering context around metrics has been mentioned several times, and it is worth noting an example when evaluating bounce rate. When bounce rate is high, the immediate impulse with this metric is to conclude that the page has a problem, and that content on the page needs to be optimized for the audience. However, it should also be considered that if some or all of the audience being delivered to the page is not "qualified" as potential converters, a high bounce rate may not be a reflection on content effectiveness, but could instead be a reflection on ineffective targeting and acquisition. As always, when evaluating under-performing metrics, all realistically possible patterns of cause and effect should be identified and then evaluated.

Conversion metrics are the backbone of our descriptive analytics, telling us whether or not our earned channels are "converting" our visitors to our key business and marketing objectives. Typically, the KPIs associated with our business objectives will be defined here as "goals", and when possible, goals should be assigned financial value. Aside from the rate of user/visitor conversion to our KPIs within any given channel, conversion measurement may also include measurement of the contribution that other channels make in driving that conversion through 'attribution' measurement that recognizes that our main or "macro" conversions may be assisted by other channels for key "micro" conversions through awareness and consideration stages leading up to the macro conversion.

Conversion: Cost per Acquisition and Return on Marketing Investment

The cost per acquisition (CPA) metric brings us to the business results of our conversion-driving efforts. To arrive at the CPA (or other conversion action), paid media costs are added to all other marketing costs before that total cost is divided by the number or value of acquisitions that occurred in the period influenced by that marketing. As with any "cost-per" metric, the lower the result the better. Also, this ratio metric simply evaluates the efficiency of how our strategy is working, it does not explain how or why any single tactic or the overall combination of tactics is delivering conversions effectively or not. That must be determined with contextual analysis behind this performance measurement.

Return on marketing investment (ROMI) quantifies the percent of return of our overall marketing budget spent across all tactics in terms of total profit. So for example, let's say Icculus Industries spent $50,000 on marketing tactics that resulted in $250,000 in instrument sales, with a total cost of $100,000 in making and shipping all the instruments. The ROMI here would be ((250-100-50)/50) which comes to a 200% ROMI.

The challenge with either cost-per-action (acquisition, conversion, etc.) or ROMI is their inherent assumption that everything that "caused" the results is captured in the costs. The ROMI calculation above is saying that $50,000 spent on marketing caused $100,000 in profit. If every aspect of a consumer's engagement with Icculus Industries is accounted for in the marketing, production, and shipping costs, and if there were no other possible drivers of conversion than those accounted for in the marketing cost, then this is accurate. But, for example, what if there was some free national publicity that helped to raise awareness? ROMI implies that the profits were only gained by what was paid for. As with CPA, the straightforward calculation of ROMI provides a directional sense of whether marketing contributed positively to results and by how much, but to make sure we have the full picture of what drove results, the analysis must be conducted with a complete context of the consumer experience.

Cross-channel Attribution

Cross-channel attribution is a method used in conjunction with cross-channel data to understand how all of our marketing channels are working together, and which are doing the most work.

The basis for that decision in a single channel like paid display, or across multiple channels, comes from a (machine learning based) understanding of how prior converters who either (1) shared a similar path to this point or (2) are significantly similar to this person at this point ultimately proceeded from this point to a conversion. Not only can the model compare and evaluate large numbers of paths through multiple channels with regard to the respective conversion value of each, but it can also predict how much each channel contributed by evaluating the probability that the same outcome could have occurred with at least one of the channels removed.

Figure 8.1
Attribution —
Paths to
Conversion

An example of how the attribution algorithm "thinks" can be seen in Figure 8.1. The figure shows three different customers' paths to a decision to buy or not. (In this case, let's say a cart left abandoned for over 30 days is considered a lost sale).

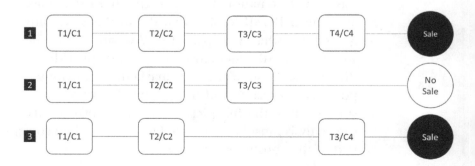

We see that customer 1 had four interactions with the brand, in four different channels, and ultimately made a purchase. Customers 2 and 3 each had just three interactions with the brand, and while customer 3 purchased, customer 2 did not. We see that customers 1 and 3 who both purchased also both engaged in channel 4, while customer 2, who did not purchase, also did not engage in channel 4.

Now, our attribution modeling algorithm will not determine that channel 4 is an important driver of purchase (thus earning a higher attribution credit) because it was present in 100% of purchases and absent from 100% of lost sales, or that channel 3 deserves less attribution credit because it was only present in 50% of sales from a sample of just three observations, but it will begin to make these determinations as it collects thousands of observations, ultimately resulting in a weighting of each channel's apparent influence over purchase in the context of all other channels that were also engaged by users and did or did not contribute to purchase in some number of cases.

This fills in one piece of the puzzle regarding our prediction as to the propensity that a customer we encounter in a channel will have to purchase if we engage them effectively in that channel, but it is only a piece of the puzzle, because these predictions come from a mean frequency of occurrence of combinations of channels against all of our observed cases, and can be made more precise when we move from the general case which ignores much of the context around this path through the channels to more specific cases that account for more context.

8.3 ACAP Section Three: Data Visualization

The purpose of analysis is to identify patterns and provide explanations for those patterns in ways that inform actions to optimize desired outcomes. Given this purpose, good analysis should provide readers with a quick understanding of an important pattern, clear insight into key drivers of the pattern, and immediate guidance in how to respond to this information.

Visualization of data and analysis taps into the human preference for visual stimulus and therefore provides a potentially powerful approach to establishing and interpreting patterns. A formula for creating valuable visualization has been presented by John Stasko, a Professor in the School of Interactive Computing at the Georgia Institute of Technology. Professor Stasko proposes that the value of visualization (V) is as follows:

$$V = \text{Time} + \text{Insights} + \text{Essence} + \text{Confidence}$$

This model asks analysts to consider four key factors in deciding whether a visualization approach is the right way to present your data. The first value in this model is *time*, or more precisely, the extent to which a visualization can help reduce the time required to answer a range of questions about the data. In a conference presentation in which this model was presented to the public, Stasko lists the types of tasks whose effort can be reduced via visualization including retrieving values, sorting and applying filters, calculating values, determining range and distribution, exposing anomalies, and illuminating clusters and correlations.

The second value in the model is *insight*, the delivery of which is of course the primary purpose of any type of analysis. Professor Stasko observes that good insights can be characterized by the extent to which they are complex, qualitative, and perhaps most importantly, unexpected, or challenging to prior conceptions and understandings, providing an "aha" moment around a problem that may have seemed inexplicable or impenetrable prior to the insight.

Next in the value of visualization comes the extent to which the visualization captures the *essence* of the data. It would appear that an ability to distill a number of variables or factors into an essential picture would result from a maximization of the time element of this equation, and would be a key driver of the insights that could be drawn from the visualization. The chief take-away here is that to capture the essence of the data, the visualization must provide both an understanding of salient details along with a view of the big picture. There is a tendency for analysts to begin "drilling down" for insights, and to drill so far that context around the analysis becomes lost (e.g. finding a pattern in the movement of a single stock without considering movement within its industry, or the market at large). The capability to deliver "aha" insights comes from providing the big picture within the data and a detailed cross-section at the same time.

The last factor in this equation is the *confidence* that the visualization inspires, as clearly the visualization will have no value if its readers do not trust the data or the analyst. Trust in an analyst is established over time, and trust in data typically follows trust in the analyst. With that said, any time a visualization or analysis of any sort challenges preconceptions, it stands subject to doubt. This creates a conundrum for the analyst; our primary objective is to create "aha" moments giving unexpected insights from the data what challenge preconceptions, but we must recognize that challenging preconceptions can create doubt that must be overcome through a method of presentation that establishes confidence. The analyst who creates "aha" insights but does not recognize the importance of confidence in analysis and the effect of challenges to the status quo on confidence may develop amazing insights that no one uses, which is an unfortunate position to be in. Balancing the insight produced with a recognition of the response it will receive and a plan to address questions of confidence rising from that response will be able to continue delivering unexpected insights that people will welcome and act upon.

An example of the wrong way to present visualization with devastating consequences comes from the tragic Challenger Space Shuttle launch. Setting aside the handwritten nature, the visualization below violates several of the variables in the $V = T + I + C + E$ approach to visualization.

Figure 8.2 shows a visualization produced by a group of engineers seeking to cancel the launch of the Challenger space shuttle in the lead up to that tragic, fatal launch. The engineer's valid concern was that a part called an "O Ring" had been known to malfunction at lower temperatures, and the temperature at launch was expected to be low enough to cause a malfunction. The engineers conducted their analysis and produced the results as shown in Figure 8.2. As we know, this information was not

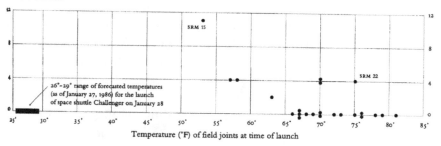

Figure 8.2 Challenger Pre-launch Analysis

enough to convince the launch managers to delay the launch, and on January 28, 1986 the shuttle blew apart 73 seconds into its flight, killing all seven of its crew.

This is a case in which the value of visualization was critical. Granted, in 1986 the engineers did not have the benefit of the data visualization capabilities we have today, but let's evaluate where the value of their visualization was diminished such that their warnings were not conveyed as well as they might have been.

This analysis does fulfill the "time" requirement for value in visualization, saving the reader from the requirement of pulling and sorting the history of O Ring damage for themselves. Where the visualization fails is in its conveyance of "insights" and "essence". The key insight that might have stopped the launch would have been an analysis of how extensive O Ring damage could lead to the entire craft exploding, and a prediction of the likelihood of O Ring damage given the temperature. The insight delivered in the analysis above could be argued to show that more O Ring damage has occurred at temperatures above 60 degrees than below 60 degrees. It also could be argued to show that launches can be successful even with O Ring damage. Thus, the insight that was meant to challenge the status quo was not effectively delivered through this visualization. Additionally, this data fails to convey the essence of the data. It fails to put the salient details in the context of the most relevant aspect of the big picture; the extreme difference in damage caused at the temperature below 55 degrees compared to damage caused above that temperature, and the lack of experience with a launch at temperatures below 50 degrees. By even using just an "average" degree of damage at each decreasing 5 degree range instead of showing all damage rankings, the increasing level of damage as temperatures dropped would have been much more apparent, and the lack of data at the range in which the launch was taking place might have been much more apparent.

The engineers who prepared this visualization tried their best, and I credit them immensely for their effort. Their ability to establish the "confidence" value for their visualization was beyond their control due to filters and biases in their organization. Some very common drivers of organizational "groupthink" — familiarity, social proof, and escalation of commitment — were amplified in what was characterized as "Go Fever" surrounding this (and every other) impending launch. Cutting through this Go Fever would have required a heroic effort at data presentation that unfortunately these engineers did not have the time or tools to deliver.

Flipping now to the other side of the coin, we will go even further back in history to look at what is widely considered to be the grandfather of all visualizations and an example of value in all four areas; a map of a cholera outbreak in London produced by John Snow in 1854 (Figure 8.3).

John Snow was a doctor in London when a Cholera outbreak struck the city in 1854. At the time, the cause of Cholera was still unknown, with many different (incorrect) theories existing around how diseases spread. Snow went to the impacted area and began to collect data, and his analysis of the data helped him determine that the common factor among all of the cases he observed was that they had all consumed water drawn from a single well (on Broad Street). He quickly conveyed his findings to authorities who removed the handle from the well. After his analysis had been responded to, Snow created the above illustration to visualize his analysis. Clearly, this visualization provides value around time saved in data collection and analysis. The insight is conveyed through an effective capturing of the essence of the data; showing the details of cases in the context of the bigger picture map of the surrounding area. And as evidenced by the fact that

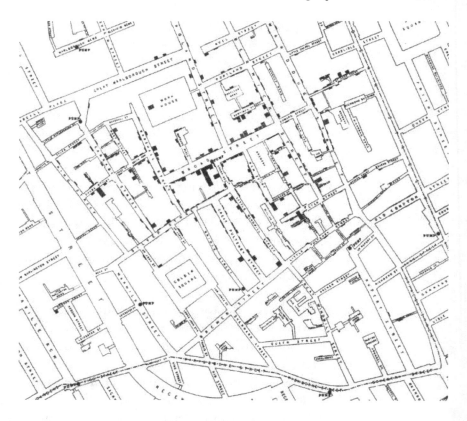

Figure 8.3
John Snow
London
Cholera Map

Snow's analysis was acted upon ever before the visualization was produced, it seems that consumers of Snow's analysis had great confidence in him.

The implications of the approach taken to visualization are clear. Valuable visualization saves time in processing data, conveys an unexpected insight, captures the essence of a large dataset by showing detail in the context of the big picture, and does so in a way that instills confidence, while less valuable visualization misses on one or all of these points.

Chapter NINE
Getting Ahead of the Game

9.1 ACAP Section 4: Data Management and Data Application

The "Data Management" section of the ACAP is where we provide details about the approach we will take to managing and using data from our various first party channels and third party sources. This section is where we will outline how we will obtain data from our website, mobile apps, social media, email, search engine optimization (SEO), search engine marketing (SEM), and paid media, and what that data will be.

In this section we will document the formats in which data will be accessed or extracted from each channel, how we will transform the data for our reporting needs and for the analytics and other applications for which this data will be used, and where we will load that data to reside as a single source of truth.

9.2 Data Management

Extract, Transform, and Load

Each of the tactics for communications presented in this book are distinct sources of data. So if we were deploying communications through every tactic discussed in earlier chapters with just one publishing intermediary per tactic, our mission in this section would be to define how to bring 20 sources of data together into a single source of truth about what we are spending, who we are reaching, and how people are responding in terms of in-channel engagement, cross-channel pathing, and our ultimate conversion measure. Large media campaigns may use multiple intermediaries for many communications tactics, increasing the sources of data that need to be integrated for the effective use of data in reporting and analytics.

Our first step in our documentation and then in practice is to identify the ways in which we can *extract* data from each of the source systems. There will be two basic options. The first will be an application programming interface (API) which will give us a direct connection to programmatically pull data from the source system's data repository into ours. The second option involves exporting data from the source system into files which are then later loaded into our system. In the case of API extraction, we are able to write centralized code that pulls data into our system from the external systems with APIs. In the case of file extraction, we need to conduct an export from each source system as a data file, which is saved to a folder where the files can be accessed for further processing. When considering the systems being used to drive communications, the evaluation of how easy it will be to extract data via API or the ability to automate file export should be a key factor in the evaluation. In the ACAP, we should list each system that contains data we want to access, and define whether it will be accessed by API or by file transfer.

In both cases, we should also list which fields we will be accessing and transferring to our single source of data.

Before we load data from APIs or files into our integrated data repository, we will almost definitely need to *transform* much of the data. In some cases, this will be to standardize the contents of fields so that once they reach our database, what was unique to the way the data for a field was stored in each source system is now common for all data in that field. For example, some systems may use "male" and "female" to denote gender while others use "M" and "F", or may use "NULL" while others use "N/A" and others use "0". There are numerous ways that the values in each data source for a common field may be unique. Within our ACAP, this section is the opportunity to identify those differences and how they will be standardized. We will also design transformation processes to cleanse and prepare the data, i.e. that find and remove duplicate records or that make sure that fields types are correct for the target dataset (i.e. that fields being loaded to a numeric field are only numbers).

The data transformation process is also where rules will be applied. Data in a single column may be split into multiple columns for the target dataset (e.g. a date and time field may be split into one date field and one time field). Data from multiple tables may be joined together around a shared column (i.e. web visit data for a user ID will be joined with sales system data for the same user ID). A new field may be created from a calculation, such as a new "sales profit" field created by the subtraction of the sum of values in the existing "sales costs" field from the sum of values in the existing "sales revenue" field. The ACAP Section 4 documentation should capture all of the data transformation design that has been built into our process.

Finally, with our data fully prepared for our target source, we are ready to *load* it to that source. The preparation of the ACAP allows us to determine the best destination for our data, which will be based on considerations like how large our dataset will become, how frequently we will access it, how complex that access will be, and how quickly we want our retrieval of data to perform. Our load process rules will define what data is overwritten with each load, and what data is appended into new rows. The load process should include validation and error handling rules, which will alert the owner of the ETL process if anything does not make its way into the database as planned.

Consumer Profiles

For the conversion scientist, a particular area of interest in the transformation process is the linkage of data around a unifying customer ID. The challenge in building a universal customer profile begins with the nature of device-constrained data collection. In web and mobile analytics, anonymous data about a user is tied to a browser, so that a single person visiting a site in the morning from a PC and in the afternoon from their phone will appear to be two different people with two different visitor IDs to the analytics system. While they will both be collected in owned data systems, their entry from a click on a content ad several days ago will not be tied to their email ID in determining what promotion they should be sent. Their unsubscribe from the email list will not be tied with their identity for retargeting rules, or with either their web or mobile visitor ID. Their like of a paid post on Facebook will not be connected to their other behavior in response to display ads or web activity. And perhaps most disturbingly for the brand, despite having taken some or all of these actions over the past few days, none of these "signals" about their experience and intentions will be recognized or acknowledged when this person finally contacts the call center for the purpose that their prior actions might indicate where they were able to be analyzed (e.g. as a highly qualified prospect for a specifically searched product, or as a dissatisfied customer awaiting a very late shipment, etc.).

In the example above, a design to create a unified customer data profile from all first-party interactions would allow the brand to recognize that this is one single person engaging in different ways across multiple channels over time, allowing the brand to anticipate this person's interests and needs and to make their best effort to address those interests and needs (and the prior activity around them) at each next point of engagement. The better the brand is at addressing interests, the more satisfied the customer or prospect, and the more likely they are to convert (or repeat, renew, refer, or upgrade).

Establishing the unified customer view in a system like a customer data platform (CDP) requires careful data design to establish a universal identifier that works across all channels. This is most easily achieved in owned touchpoints that allow login against something like a customer ID, which will associate each touchpoint specific ID (e.g. laptop browser visitor ID and mobile browser visitor ID) with each other via the shared customer ID, usually coordinated within our CDP. This approach would also tie these touchpoints to the customer relationship management (CRM) system containing the customer ID, and to a call center call that asks for a customer ID (or links to that ID via a customer phone number). From the call center, a purchase, or a registration/login, we may also connect an email address with this customer ID.

Integrating our owned channels in an experience that requires some kind of authentication requires planning to design each channel's experience to collect a common identifying variable in each of these multiple channels and effort in the integration of those multiple channel data sources via that field, but with a commitment to that design and integration effort, the path to integration is relatively clear. The next challenge arises in the effort to expand this integration to the inclusion of paid and social media impressions and engagement.

With the connections we've made above through our owned media, we can understand the user by their behavior across all of our owned channels, and by all the information we have about them within our CRM database, which can include demographic and transactional data. We can augment this with additional demographics and data about each user's perceived interests and actual engagement with context across the web through our DMP, which links any user we've encountered and tagged (pairing their unique DMP ID with our CDP universal ID) in owned or paid (DSP) media to all of the information the DMP compiles about them from other third-party data sources (anonymized offline transaction data, anonymized paid media impression/engagement data, etc.).

Information about a specific person's response to our advertising can be provided via a DSP which pairs our universal customer ID with that individual's unique DSP ID. With these additions, we can understand any individual currently present in any of our paid or owned channels in terms of their prior impressions on paid channels. We may also attempt to pair a social profile with the universal customer ID by asking for a social profile or social sign-up in various channels that are already associated with the universal customer ID.

Consumer Privacy

The first edition of this book, published in 2016, had several pages devoted to the possibilities for data collection available from the Facebook app permissions of the time. One of the permissions that the book noted users could grant to the maker of any third-party Facebook app as they authenticated for the first time was the permission to "access my friend's information". This permission allowed the third-party app maker (which could be anyone) to access and analyze each of the authenticated user's friend's information, including their likes, statuses, and all the other content they made available to their friends. This meant that at the time that book was published, one user could give permission to any app maker to access and analyze information for tens to hundreds of the user's friends, without those others knowing such information was being accessed and analyzed.

Access and use of personal information was still very wide-open at that time due to an extreme lack of awareness among the general population about the amount of information they were creating about themselves through social media analytics and apps and the ways in which that was available to others. There was also a general lack of awareness about the more behind-the-scenes ways in which their digital behaviors and online and offline transactions were being tracked, analyzed, and sold so that they could be classified and targeted.

The aftermath of the 2016 US elections was the wake-up call for many people around the capabilities of data analysis and its application to content targeting. In 2018, investigative journalism brought the firm Cambridge Analytica (CA) into public view. The firm bought data from an app called "This is Your Digital Life" which requested the "access my friend's information" permission from users. Around 270,000 Facebook users authenticated to this app with those permissions, and according to reports, the result was access to over 87 million Facebook users' information.

Access to that much information without the permission of those individuals might create concern on its own. What disturbed the public more was the understanding of what was done with that data. The information about people's connections and interests and passions and locations that was available from Facebook allowed CA to develop highly specific segments around people's motivational drivers. It refined those segments with its own survey research. It then used those segments to develop content that would resonate most strongly with consumers' personality and motivations, and used digital targeting to steer that content to those whom it wanted to persuade to its clients' interests. (Its clients were mostly political candidates and movements around the world, including then candidate Donald Trump and parts of the "Brexit" movement in the UK.)

The only illegality in the US related to what CA did was its use of Facebook data purchased from a third party, and it was actually the app maker that had violated terms of service with Facebook. Facebook still banned CA from advertising on its platform due to what it felt was deception around how it had been developing targets, and CA closed its doors in 2018. However, despite being a visible pioneer, CA was not alone in the practice of developing psychological profiles from what data consumers shared about themselves and matching that to other digital records for profile enrichment, content personalization, and highly refined targeting, and these practices continue, though as a matter of survival, now with stricter attention to compliance to data protection regulations.

In the time that has passed since the first edition of this book, the European Union implemented the General Data Protection Regulation (GDPR) which it had passed in 2016 around the time of publication of the first edition, and California passed and implemented the California Consumer Privacy Act (CCPA), both of which are focused on the use and protection of individuals' personally identifiable information, including each person's right to know who has their data, to understand how it is being used, and to control that use, including forbidding the resale of personal data or requiring the deletion of personal data. Following the CA revelations, Facebook had already begun tightening the access to information it allowed through permissions limiting the possibility of another CA-type PR incident through its platform, and the GDPR and CCPA legally ensure that such secret access and distribution of such widespread personal information is no longer permissible. But these corporate moves and governmental regulations do not prohibit the type of work CA was doing if it is conducted by a new set of rules.

Having learned how quickly things develop and change in less than a half-decade, I will not get deep into the CCPA and GDPR in these pages, as there will likely be addendums and additions to the regulations around data protections that may be more relevant by the time you read this. What does matter about these regulations — what they have in common and what will be the foundation for further and more specific regulations — is what they seek to accomplish.

Both regulations give individual citizens the right to know when data is being collected, what data has been collected, and what happened to that data. They give consumers the right to have data removed from a system. The type of data they focus on puts both first-party data in a CRM or CDP systems (of over 50,000 records) in any business under the jurisdiction of these regulations as well as all data aggregators and resellers. They both exclude the regulation of consumer traits, behaviors, or transactions that are anonymized, deidentified, or aggregated — which leaves digital advertising models largely intact.

Obviously, any business keeping digital records of consumers and their transactions should always have been concerned with protecting that data from theft, but these regulations put legal ramifications behind what had been merely an ethical and PR concern. Any business holding personally identifiable data on consumers should be prepared to receive and comply with requests for information on what is held about them, and further requests to purge information about them.

What these regulations do not accomplish is any sort of simplification around data collection and usage from the standpoint of consumers' self-management. Through what seem like standard interactions with everything from their app installs to their internet provider to their logged-in websites to their loyalty program memberships and credit card applications, the average consumer has "opted-in" to provide their data to a wider array of sources than they are typically aware.

And the type of data consumers are sharing continues to race ahead of consumers' realization of the fact. During the writing of this edition in 2019, investigative journalism by the *New York Times* turned up a data file containing 50 billion location pings of the phones of 12 million Americans. These phones can be linked with specific individuals, and tracked to specific locations. This investigative report was able to identify visitors to the Playboy Mansion, to the

Pentagon, and to protest marches, to name just a few potentially sensitive locations. While the CCPA would allow California residents to manage this information if they knew it existed, the investigation rightly observed that most consumers do not know the names of the companies that collect this information, if they happen to know that such information is being collected at all.

Continually evolving capabilities in data storage and machine learning algorithms will continue to expand the personally identifiable data that can be collected, stored, and matched with other datasets. While consumers and regulators perhaps begin to grapple with the implications of location tracking, another front has opened around facial recognition, where private data management companies provide storage for images of individuals and allow matching of these images to other information about the individuals, including other images.

The uses of facial recognition data and the implications they have for individual privacy will continue to evolve ahead of regulation and oversight until they likely reach a point similar to the CA case for social media data, after which we can expect another form of data collection (perhaps commercial DNA data?) will begin the cycle. The aim of this book is not to predict specifically what data will come next, but to share the certainty that as long as new types of data can be collected, they will, and that analytics will be applied to this data to find patterns that can be leveraged to guide individuals toward desired actions. Also, there will be applications of the results of analysis that fall well beyond most people's ethical comfort zone, because there is always a portion of the business world that sees the lack of ethics as a competitive advantage.

So the most important prediction I can apply in these pages is in this plea to each reader: given your interest in the topic of this book, you may find yourself at a crossroads that shapes whether people are increasingly placed under privately maintained surveillance and subject to manipulation by forces they don't understand within an unequitable information dynamic, or whether our marketplace for ideas and goods is conducted under information parity. If you face such a choice, I urge you to maintain the stance that is better aligned with the ethics of a fair and open society.

9.3 Data Application: Predictive, Prescriptive, and Adaptive Analytics

Predictive Analytics and Machine Learning

With the ethics of how we use data to shape consumer behavior in mind, we turn to the analytics that allow us to identify those factors that will most likely shape behaviors toward our desired goals. The importance and value of prediction to marketing efforts has been stated repeatedly throughout these pages, but perhaps three key benefits are worth repeating.

1. Predictions can be made during planning to optimize inputs to the consumer journey in terms of optimal initial allocations to channels, content, and user experience as determined by a forecast of results.

2. Predictions can be made during the delivery of the consumer journey to identify and rank prospects (new customer or existing cross/up sell, renewal, etc.) and their propensity to convert.
3. Predictions can be made during the delivery of the consumer journey to deliver the best content for a consumer based on how well we expect it will drive revenue, cost per conversion, or some other key performance indicator (KPI).

Put in the simplest terms, a prediction is an estimate or forecast of a future outcome based on knowledge of the past. The best way to establish these forecasts about the future is to identify factors that have occurred in the past that appear to have influenced the outcome we are seeking to predict.

The most common method for making predictions is to review the statistical average and variance from a history of earlier observations and expect a similar pattern to be sustained into the future. This approach can reveal how patterns change across different time periods and under different circumstances. For example, average sales might typically increase in October through mid-December, so we might predict that this will happen again in the coming year.

Regression modeling is a more sophisticated approach to prediction which uses an equation to explain, or model, the interactions between independent variables in relation to the dependent outcome. The most straightforward approach to regression is the *linear regression* model, which fits the mean of a predicted linear and continuous range of outcomes as closely as possible to the set of observed outcomes based on the distance of the mean of each predicted outcome from the means of the observed outcomes surrounding it. When the dependent variable is not continuous but discrete and bounded, *logistic regression* may be used to transform the variable to a continuous range.

Machine learning allows analysts to let software programs try different approaches to problem solving, to "learn" what works best by evaluating the accuracy of the outcomes. Machine learning can be supervised, in which case the software sees the results and tries to uncover the rules that create the results. Or it can be unsupervised, in which case the software receives only inputs and looks for the most convincing patterns related to those inputs. A common example of unsupervised modeling is the cluster analysis we discussed in Chapter 4.

An analyst may look to supervised machine learning when the order in which the dependent future events will occur matters to our analysis. Regression is not able to find the temporal or sequential structure of independent variables. In these cases, *time-series* approaches to prediction include autoregressive models, moving average models, and the combination of these such as ARIMA (autoregressive integrated moving average models). Analysts should recognize the need for time-series analysis if the sequence of events in a prediction matters to the conclusions we will draw and actions we will take.

Another machine learning method commonly applied to conversion analysis, *Classification and Regression Trees* (*CART*) analysis, produces predictions using a decision tree approach (Figure 9.1).

Figure 9.1
CART
Visualization

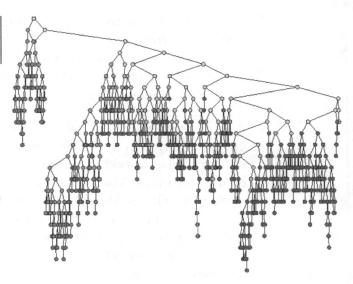

The random forest model is a common example of this approach.

In this approach, a number of individual probabilistic decision trees are constructed and the mean or mode prediction of the individual trees is presented as the prediction. This model accounts much better for multiple potential next steps in a series of steps than does regression, and as such is suited to the third purpose defined above; predicting how a sequence of interactions across channels can be optimized toward potential revenue, cost per conversion, or some other KPI.

Prescriptive and Adaptive Analytics: Neural Networks

As mentioned in an earlier chapter, prescriptive analytics simply adds the question of "why" to the "what" and "how much" of predictive analytics. The need for prescriptive analytics is reached when the big data in our possession explain a past that is different from the future we expect, or when we have not accrued enough information to clearly establish predictions around cause and effect. This shift in the use of machines from passively processing predictive models to actively developing better models moves us up the analytics pyramid from predictive analytics to prescriptive and adaptive analytics.

Neural networks are the coolest sounding and most recognized method of prescriptive and adaptive analytics/machine learning. This method for machine learning is supported through a computational approach called *gradient descent.*

Neural network models take a variety of input variables and pass them through an adaptive weighting process to find the combination of adaptively weighted inputs that best align outputs from the model with outputs from the training data.

This approach is built on structure of individual "perceptrons", which act like neurons in a real brain, taking some input, processing it, and firing the output to the next neuron (Figure 9.2).

Let's say we want to train our machine learning algorithm to make an offer when it recognizes a person who is an existing customer and does not currently have an item in their basket or a person who has an item in their basket but is not an existing customer.

Figure 9.2
Neural Network
"Perceptron"

Figure 9.3
"And"
Condition

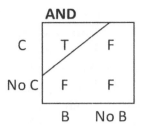

Figure 9.4
"Or"
Condition

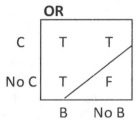

We could try to evaluate this with simple rules such as "AND" and "OR", which will produce linearly separable results. Figures 9.3 and 9.4 illustrate what is meant by this.

Let's place "basket (B)" and "no basket (No B)" on the X axis, and "customer (C)" and "not customer (No C)" on the Y axis. If we evaluate customers who are a customer AND have an item in their basket, we get the following linearly separable result, meaning that the division between the condition that meets the criteria and the conditions that don't can be divided with a straight line. The only true result is produced when both conditions are met.

We can equally evaluate whether any given person is either a customer or has an item in their basket, with the only false result being when a visitor has neither an item in their basket, nor is a customer.

Neither of these linearly separable results allow us to recognize someone who is a customer but does not have an item in their basket, or a person who is not a customer but does have an item in their basket. Put into logical expression, such a condition is known as an "exclusive or", or "XOR" (Figure 9.5).

A simple neural network will help us find this result.

Figure 9.6 shows a very simple neural network processing our two inputs "X" and "Y". In the middle layer, known as the "hidden layer", at the top we have a perceptron processing the "AND" rule, and at the bottom, one processing the "OR" rule. In the scenario above, the "X" perceptron receives four stimuli; "Basket, No Basket, Basket, No Basket". The "Y" perceptron received four corresponding stimuli; "Customer, Customer, Not a Customer, Not a Customer". In response to evaluating for "customer AND basket" for each pair, the top "AND" perceptron outputs "true, false, false, false". And in response

Figure 9.5
"XOR"
Condition

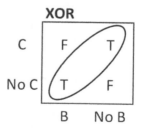

Figure 9.6
Neural
Network
Decision

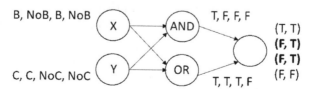

to evaluating for "customer OR basket" for each pair, the "OR" perceptron outputs "true, true, true, false". When these pairs are combined in the output perceptron, the combinations find the "exclusive OR" condition: the two cases where the outputs do not match.

This is a very simple approach to a neural network. There can be, and typically are, more than two inputs. In one marketing application we might provide a visitor's gender, prior visit status, customer status, days since last purchase, and current type of interaction. It is this ability to provide any combination of factors as input for a decision that makes neural networks so powerful.

One important element of the way neural networks process that was not mentioned above is the weighting they provide to each exchange from perceptron to perceptron. This weighting is how neural networks adjust their "understanding" of a combination of inputs to "learn". Weighting was not shown in the example above because the simple nature of the problem made the need for weights unnecessary. However, let us now consider that each of our results is being used to predict a binary outcome to purchase or not, noted as 0 or 1. Let us say that True outputs from our hidden layer are given a value of 1, and False outputs are given a value of 0. Finally, say that each output from the hidden layer carries a weight of 0.5. Let's look at our outputs, and add the actual outcome for each case as well.

We see that with the model as shown in Figure 9.7, our prediction was correct in one out of four cases, and halfway correct in another. With this

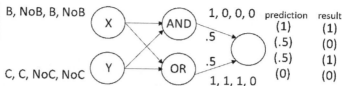

Figure 9.7
Weighted
Neural Network
Decision

information, our model could adjust weights. In this case, for our understanding, we will adjust only the weights shown above, but an actual network would adjust weights from the inputs to the hidden layer, and would contain an "error" or "bias" perceptron, the weight of which could also be adjusted. For our purposes, this network would likely adjust the weighting for the "AND" output down, and the weighing for "OR" up. If they were weighted (0.75, 0.25), then the output would be (1, 0.75, 0.75, 0). We have not improved our prediction for the second actual occurrence, rather we have increased our error. To fix this error, the network would weight the input into the hidden layer, giving higher weight to the "X" inputs than the "Y" inputs, and would continue reweighting at every layer of the network until the predicted outputs were optimized in alignment with the actual outcomes against which the network was being "trained".

One of the most popular methods by which neural networks and other machine learning algorithms "learn", e.g. adjust the weights of each connection, is an optimization method called gradient descent, through which local minima (for an optimized cost function or utility function) are established.

Figure 9.8 represents a multidimensional "decision space" — capable of taking on any number of dimensions. In the diagram above, the algorithm has

Figure 9.8
Decision
Space

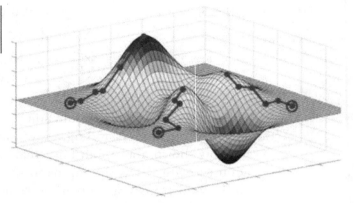

set three starting points then evaluated the steps needed to take to move from each starting point (error, shown by the height dimension) to the local optimum (the point at which a single step in any direction will not lead to further decent).

Neural networks "learn" or receive training via gradient decent algorithms, which adjust the weights in the hidden layer via gradient descent until each node in the hidden layer has found the weighting which works in conjunction with weighting in every other node in that layer to the optimal reduction of error in the model.

Machine leaning algorithms are useful in the dynamic delivery of content, whether within planning and budgeting scenarios, programmatic targeting and retargeting, or personalized user experience delivery.

Chapter TEN

Content Creates Cultural Experience

Analytics is more than just data. Great analysis requires transformation of data to information, of information to knowledge, and hopefully, over time, of knowledge to wisdom. This final chapter is an attempt to share perspectives on our society and the culture of businesses as new sources of knowledge which will hopefully be transformed into wisdom around the practice of analytics.

10.1 The Information Society: Media Cycles and Feedback Loops

In the first chapter of this book, you were introduced to Marshall McLuhan's concept of hot and cold media, which implies the power of media to change the environment around it in a sensorial way. But beyond the senses, McLuhan's theory is one of the impact of temperature change on the environment, specifically in terms of expansion and contraction; some new communications media cause culture to "heat up" until either some aspect of culture "melts down" or a countervailing cool medium emerges to cool things down. But what does it mean to "heat up" and "cool down"?

A "hot" medium is one that engages multiple senses as completely as possible, and requires very little "reading", interpretation, or completion by the receiver. McLuhan observes that a completely hot medium essentially evokes a type of hypnosis in the receiver, and offers early "big band" jazz with its intricate composed and conducted scores and its associated "Jitterbug" dance as examples of "hot" media. Conversely, a "cool" medium is one that carries very little information on its own, and requires the receiver to interpret and/or complete the message. McLuhan proposes that a completely cool medium would evoke pure fantasy/hallucination, as the receiver must provide every aspect of information. As an example of "cool" media, McLuhan suggests the evolution of jazz into its "cool" stage (yep — you're seeing the cycle emerge), with its freeform flow and long, improvised solos, and the emergence of unstructured dances like the Twist, which did away with the intricate coding of the Jitterbug and let dancers improvise as they liked, bringing their own interpretation to the music. Mirrored sunglasses have always been "cool" as a communication medium because they require the receiver to complete the face/expression of the wearer, while the latest fashions (the tighter the better) are always the "hottest" thing — because they add information about the wearer (e.g. that they have "currency" in physical, cultural, and financial terms).

McLuhan's book offers an incredible array of examples in the cultural impacts of 20th century hot and cool media, so I encourage you to add it to your reading list. What these examples illustrate very convincingly is that "the medium is the message". Perhaps you've encountered this phrase before and were possibly aware that it comes from McLuhan. Taken without the context of the book, it still intrinsically makes a certain kind of sense, but it makes much more sense when considered in the context of media, hot and cool. In this context one can observe that if effective sustained communication requires the constant interplay of "hot" and "cool" media to keep a balanced temperature (to avoid cultural melt-downs and freeze-ups), then "the message" embedded in any medium is its cultural "temperature"; does it shout or whisper? Does it hypnotize or cause hallucinations? Does its temperature depend on complimentary or conjoined media?

McLuhan observed that broadcast television was primarily a "hot" medium, with its rapidly paced plots and pacing, its laugh-tracks and scores and its interspersed intense bursts of advertising providing strong emotional cues and leaving no time to consider what's just been seen or what's coming next. This notion of television as a "hypnotizing" force seemed to resonate, becoming a very strong cultural meme that persists today. Unfortunately, McLuhan died long before the internet took its current form and social networks created a new form of cultural interaction, because his take on these new media would have certainly helped us understand not just how technology is shaping society, but more importantly for the innovators among us, what is likely to come next in terms of communication technology based on the culture's need to "heat" or "cool" what has come before. While I certainly cannot claim McLuhan's insight, I can attempt to extend his framework against the media that have emerged since McLuhan's last observation.

Let There Be Browsers

Newsgroups/Bulletin Boards/Email (Cool): At the beginning of what has become our contemporary digital media landscape, the early internet was a very cool medium. Everything was text based, and communication was not nearly as instantaneous as it is today, messages were posted on "boards" in groups or sent via email and typically waited for response until the receiver accessed the board or account and saw the message. While it was possible to share files, nothing could be viewed immediately, but required download (very slow over dial-up modems) and frequently also decompression. In short, the reader had to bring a lot to the medium to get to the meaning in any message.

HTML (Cool): offered a profoundly new method of non-linear writing, but despite its radical departure from linear writing, it was still primarily about writing, and the prodigious use of links on almost every word in early HTML coding meant that readers still had to do a great deal of work to uncover the full meaning embedded in an HTML-based medium.

Browser (Hot): It was the Mozilla browser that helped the web "heat-up" in the mid-1990s. The Mozilla browser allowed multi-media elements to merge with the written aspect of HTML, and guided web development away from the early practice of dispersion through links and more toward emersion through "content".

Broadband (Hot): The immersive nature (and "heating-up") of the web was exponentially expanded with the introduction of broadband/high-speed access and the emergence of animation and streaming audio. It is really no coincidence that this hot new communication technology became so overheated as to create a "bubble" in internet investment and development, which then burst in 2000–2001.

Mobile and Text (Cool): Meanwhile on a separate technological track, mobile technology was developing in a "cool" state. The emergence of smaller and smaller phones with added functionality like contacts memory, voice dialing, and most importantly text messaging was a very cool development for everyone who lived through it. Communication via voice and text were both cool in McLuhan's terms as well; conversations were frequently lost due to spotty service and really lame battery life, and text messages were written in entirely abbreviated forms, requiring readers to complete every word with omitted vowels, syllables, grammar, and punctuation.

Blogs (Cool): As the "dot-com" bubble burst, a cooler form of web communication, blogging, emerged to fill in the void. In its initial form, blogging was a very text-heavy medium built around a single page, quite a cool-down from the multi-media, multi-page website that had just melted down. In contrast to the emergence of "digital" specialty firms during the dot-com bubble, blogging brought a DIY ethic back to the web, allowing anyone and everyone to communicate anything at any time, a characteristic which lent itself (legitimately) to comedic (and occasionally tragic) criticism of the practice. While some blogs (e.g. Drudge Report, Huffington Post) took an approach that eventually led them to more legitimate "media" status on par with the digitized print outlets (e.g. NYT.com), the "Blogosphere" itself was (and is) a largely cool medium (as anyone who attempted to mine meaningful data from it in the early days can attest); a universe of poorly-written and partial communications or completely abandoned efforts with huge vacuum-filled gaps in-between.

P2P/Torrents (Cool): At this point in the early 2000s, as a new DIY ethic emerged from the excess and collapse of Web1.0, peer-to-peer file-sharing emerged as the primary point of user activity at the center of the emerging new web. Napster, a music file-sharing service was the poster-child for this new generation of software and social interaction, but sharing was not constrained to Napster. Bit Torrent software turned home computers into networked file-servers, and in conjunction with home broadband, these file-sharing applications transformed the internet from a text-delivery system into a true media platform which made previously platform-constrained and copyright protected content suddenly ubiquitous. The nature of the technology is itself the very description of a "cool" medium, fragmented pieces of content (bit packets) being assembled by the receiver into a cohesive whole.

Social Networks (Hot): With blogs leaving much to be desired from an interactivity standpoint, and with content sharing becoming the centerpiece of the new web, the cool vacuum of the post-dot-com web needed some heating up, making the environment perfect for the introduction of platforms like Friendster (2002), MySpace (2003), and ultimately Facebook. These platforms simplified posting, (lowering the expectations around posts since a sentence could suffice where blogs had seemed to want paragraphs), allowed multi-media to be easily and seamlessly integrated (reducing the complexity of installing and running torrents, though also reducing access to copyright-infringed content) and most importantly, offered ready-made audiences through the capability to find and add "friends" or connections who were willing to receive posts and contribute their own in return, both through the established network members as well as the drastically improved personal search engine opti-mization (SEO) which these networks provided (meaning Google had something it could find and show under a search on a person's name).

YouTube (Hot): The "re-heating" of the web reached a fever pitch with the expanding popularity of what was initially known as "vlogging" (for video blog-ging), and the emergence of YouTube (2005) as the center of the web's video universe. Critics derided the channel as just another vanity outlet that would shrivel up and die as the novelty wore off and people tired of dealing with video quality that was pretty bad by any standard, and the long wait times or frequent interruptions while video buffered due to the lower bandwidth connections of the time. Instead, within a short period of time, video quality improved rapidly, access to better connections expanded to a broader population, and most importantly, people went crazy for a type of video content that wasn't available any-where else.

YouTube was the birthplace for two concepts that "digital natives" take for granted today. The first is "going viral". Something about YouTube videos com-pelled people to share them with friends and acquaintances, and the most broadly (and quickly) spread videos were considered to have gone "viral", spreading from person to person until everyone has caught the fever (i.e. Numa Numa 2005).

The second concept spawned by YouTube is the widespread recognition of the "meme". The "meme" is a concept introduced by Richard Dawkins, who earlier in his career had established the concept of the "gene". Where the gene is a part of the assembly instructions for a living organism which carries instructions for how to assemble the building blocks of life, a "meme" is similarly a part of the blueprint for a culture, providing the building blocks of culture (individual minds) instructions for how to assemble together a common way of seeing or interpreting things. The "virality" of certain videos on YouTube (and subsequently everything imaginable, from "LOL cats" to "Sad Keanu") exposed the reality of the "meme" — a theme or concept that not only required some cultural knowledge for interpretation, but which also shapes or evolves a culture (or more correctly sub-culture) through its existence.

Clearly, the ability to go viral and create a feverish response to content that actually shapes culture belies the "hotness" of this new medium, which when coupled with the heat of social networks could no longer be contained on laptop and desktop computers.

iPhone (Hot): Enter the iPhone (2007). The iPhone channeled the heat from social networks and video away from the bounds of the computer monitor and into a handheld format allowing the hot and viral content of the internet to be accessed anywhere, at any time. The iPhone also marked the jump of mobile technology from cool (voice and text) to hot, and engendered the heating up of texting itself in the form of Twitter, a development that triggered a new cooling phase of digital technology.

Digital Primitivism, or the Rebirth of Cool

McLuhan observes that the aural and visual storytelling medium of pre-literate cultures was an inherently cool medium, requiring the listener to add their own interpretations to the images being painted by speech or drawing. By 2007, the heat generated by the first 15 years of expansion in digital media had jumped the bounds of even laptops on its way to becoming fully mobile and universally accessible.

The first 15 years of digital expansion had also engendered a significant cultural change; the coming into being of "digital natives", children of the developed world who since their first encounter with technology had been immersed in cable TV, then YouTube, torrents, and smart phones. More than anyone else, the "millenials" who had been born and raised in the feverish environment of digital expansion were in desperate need of some kind of cooling counterbalance in their culture. In fact, the most distinguished sub-culture among millennials around 2007 was Hipsterism, a pastiche of "retro" (or more "primitive") cultural modes of cool based primarily on beatnick (1955–1965) 1980s' pop, and grunge (1990s) styles in clothing, music, and entertainment.

Twitter (Cool)

Into this environment comes Twitter. The origin story of Twitter emerges from the center of digital "cool", the South by Southwest Interactive festival in Austin Texas. Less than a year old in March of 2007, Twitter's founders saw an opportunity to establish highly influential and technology-literate software evangelists, and by promoting their "one-to-many" messaging concept around this conference, saw their usage increase 200% over the course of a week. The Twitter experience is now well-known, 140 character messages that could be sent either to individuals (like a traditional text message) or to groups of "followers". During the 2007 conference, Twitter was rapidly adopted by attendees to build their personal social network without having to enter details into a Contact Management software or pocket a business card, since following and being followed was made easy by Twitter. And Twitter was a natural for sharing quick updates on what was happening around Austin, both in conference sessions, and more importantly, around the parties that were happening outside of the conference.

Like texting, Twitter is a cool medium, in that messages must be abbreviated and condensed. A raw Twitter stream is as close to chaos as a communication medium is likely to get — a rapidly refreshing stream of random and unconnected missives from a pool of contacts without any overarching categorization and sorting structure in place. As a means of creating some order from the chaos, Twitter's users developed their own structure with the introduction of the hashtag (#) to indicate the tweet's topic or category, and Twitter's engineers responded by generating automatic links on hashtags that search for all other tweets also carrying that hashtag.

Twitter's emergence in 2007 is inextricably linked with the iPhone's own rapid adoption and the subsequent interest in location-based communication. With mobile technology and a simplified communication medium, people seemed naturally inclined to share details about where they were and what they were doing at any given moment. However, despite its growth and popularity, Twitter usage still remained a bit of a sub-culture, with tacit and explicit rules about correct forms of engagement and interaction, and with a strong aversion to intrusion by corporations looking to tap into a highly influential audience. As a cool medium, getting engaged and staying engaged in Twitter required some effort. Many people, especially younger "digital natives" found it much more difficult to build their network in Twitter than in the "hot" Facebook network (especially since most of their friends didn't see what Twitter could give them that Facebook already didn't). Once on Twitter, separating the wheat from the chaff was difficult, and being as "cool" a medium as it was, staying engaged with followers seemed to demand a high-degree of response. So for the "digital natives", Twitter as the first wave of the new "cooling" phase was not as natural to adopt as it was for the attendees of the SxSWi conference in 2007 who likely skewed to "Gen X" who had been engaged with cool digital media before.

Tumblr (Cool)

Despite the weak attraction to Twitter as the first of the new "cool" media, millennial "digital natives" were still unknowingly "burnt out" on hot channels and in need of a cool escape. By April of 2007, in a sure sign of needing to escape from the hot expansion of the media, vintage hunting and retro-worship had become the core of "hipster" identify. In that same month, digital media felt its first cooling wave in the form of Tumblr. Like Twitter, Tumblr is a "micro-blogging" platform that was designed specifically to allow users to share content and interests in small snippets. However, unlike Twitter, but very much in keeping with the emergence and appeal to the "natives" of a more "primitive" digital communication approach, Tumblr is used primarily to share visual content rather than text. Adding to the "cool" component of Tumblr and the "primitive" tendencies it generates, a good number of the most popular Tumblr sites were dedicated to user-generated "photoshopped" pastiche images which photo-realistically portray imaginary or fantasy scenarios. The use of (as realistic as possible) visual imagery to generate humorous or serious allegorical or metaphorical reflections on reality has been a common cultural thread from the most primitive to the most cultured, and the visual medium still typically has a more effective and immediate impact on the receiver than does the written word. A picture still speaks a thousand words, and in conjunction with their fluency in cultural memes, Tumblr allowed "digital natives" to express complex and profound intellectual and emotional positions and views through snippets of imagery and text.

It is likely that as a cool respite from hot media, this use of visual signification in digital communications will expand across societies and cultures and into subsequent generations. Dr. Don Schultz of Medill IMC who travels broadly studying marketing and communications shared with me his belief that the refinement of methods for the expression and reception of ideas through images (along will ubiquitous mobile accessibility) will more broadly open the digital world to societies with large-scale illiteracy. In these cultures, image-based digital literacy will emerge as the prevailing common literacy, while traditional text-based literacy will stagnate further. The extension of the digital world, digital creation, and digital commerce to these developing nations can have a profound impact on current structures of economic and social stratification, both intra- and inter-nationally.

In more literate areas, textual literacy will continue to be a focus of general education, and written communication will never be replaced as a source and conduit of power. Undoubtedly, however, the nature and content of writing and the standard for literacy will change with subsequent generations, so that the definition of textual literacy to the graduating class of 2040 will be evolved from yet distinct (through both additions and subtractions) from what is considered literacy in 2020 (just as graduates in 1990 in meeting their standard of literacy had been through handwriting classes back in grade-school and BASIC programming language courses in middle-school that 2020 grads likely never encountered).

Pinterest (Cool)
The next popular product of the cool digital wave was Pinterest, an almost entirely visual social network where image sharing by category or interest is assumed, and text is optional. The layout of Pinterest is quite elegant and translates nicely to a tablet device (i.e. iPad or Kindle). From first use, Pinterest's user experience is highly intuitive and guidance for new users is visually driven with subordinated text.

Snapchat (Cool)
Snapchat is a logical spawn of two cool media; the
digital image and texting, and its rapid adoption by
digital natives illustrated the extent to which cool digital media were an alternative to hot media. Snapchat
is cool, taken to its extreme in digital media. It is the
anti-Facebook: a piece of content meant to last for
only a short time for a limited set of viewers before
self-destructing. No timeline, no history, no record of
any communication — just an instantaneous exchange
that disappears to make way for the next.

The Cycle Reheats

The respite from the hypnotizing continuous streams
of information that was provided by the small-bite
nature of tweets and snaps and by the visual presentation of Tumblr posts and Pinterest pins was an
anomaly in the evolutionary path of digital technology. Overall, the nature of digital is always-on, ever-
present, and overwhelming in volume; the very
definition of hot media. So the hot media innova-
tions continued.

Pandora/Last.fm/Spotify (Hot)
In 2008, the introduction of the Pandora mobile
application suddenly gave smartphone users free
and legal access to a library of music ranging from
classical to the newest rap music. This service, which
spawned follow-up mobile apps from similar services
like Last.fm and Spotify, delivers volumes of music
on a mobile device that could only have been
dreamed of at the computer download speeds, memory constraints, and copyright infringement concerns of just a few years earlier.

What was more unique about these new music sharing services than their licensing agreements and
technical architecture however, was their foundation
in "social networking". More than Pandora, Last.fm
and Spotify made sharing music and comments
across a social network a key component of their
platform. Spotify's sharing architecture, including
shared playlists and ability to share and comment on
songs or albums across friends, helped quickly erode
the lead of earlier platforms, while new alternatives
like SoundCloud emerged that offer broad direct
access to audio creators' content.

iPad (Hot)

The iPad launch in 2010 added fuel to the fire under
digital media. Over the years following the iPad's
launch, the iPad and other tablets that followed its
design became increasingly adopted, shifting more
media into the mobile space than phones alone
could deliver effectively, and shifting culture's expectation of the type of digital experience that could
be accessed and consumed while away from a computer. The integration of touchscreens into service
environments (bank, airport, dining, etc.) created
another path along which content over public
screens will be widely available for short context and
transaction based digital interactions.

Google Glass and Oculus Rift (Hot)

Google Glass launched in 2013 as a wearable display,
which extended the evolution of human–computer
interaction via a screen that was constantly affixed to
the personal view, providing real-time contextual
information to the wearer while recording the wearer's
context. In 2014, Facebook purchased Oculus Virtual
Reality (VR) and took over development of that

product, signaling how a classical hot media (Facebook) envisioned hot digital media expanding into the realm of fully immersive VR.

As of publication of the second edition, wearable Augmented Reality (AR) has not yet progressed to widespread adoption — but Google spinoff Niantic Labs, Microsoft, Magic Leap, Apple, and Facebook's Oculus (which is pursuing AR in addition to VR) are among a crowd of powerful innovators who are poised to see that AR will become widespread within the 2020s.

Streaming Video (Hot)
By 2013, the options to watch a huge array of video content without cable (or ancient DVD players and a video library) had become well established, so much so that 2013 was the first year of year-over-year subscriber losses for cable. Entering 2013 Hulu, which had launched in 2007 to offer advertising supported streaming of television programs, and Netflix, a subscription-based service that had shifted from DVD rental to streaming movies (also in 2007), had reached approximately 3 and 30 million global subscribers, respectively.

Television was designated as a hot media in McLuhan's own assessment, and what streaming video services like Hulu and Netflix (and now Amazon, Sling, YouTubeTV, HBO Now, and Disney+ to name a few more) have created is an even hotter opportunity to "binge-watch" entire seasons of programs in one sitting — leading to an even more hypnotic aspect of perhaps the hottest media around.

Twitch and Reddit (Hot)

Twitch is a unique brand of streaming video, in that its broadcasters are regular people who stream live. Twitch was initially focused on a niche group of live-streaming gamers, but saw rapid growth after it was acquired by Amazon in 2014. Twitch is still focused primarily on live gaming, with an expanding focus on creative pursuits and even talk-shows and live blogs. Importantly, Twitch allows streamers to interact live with viewers. The already hot nature of streaming content coupled with an interactive format for trash-talking and debate makes Twitch a clear apex example of the evolutionary direction of hot digital media.

Like Twitch, the online discussion forum Reddit had existed for several years before 2014. Since 2005, Reddit had provided a service that started with the same design as the internet's earliest bulletin boards, allowing participants to post content on any topic. As it developed, Reddit evolved a graphical user-interface for submission of text, images, and links. Posts can be engaged with through threaded comments, and voted up or down. It is introduced here beginning in 2014 only because the number of topical forums nearly doubled that year, and its growth since then now makes it one of the topmost visited sites in the US and the world.

As a bulletin board, Reddit would have been a cool technology. What Reddit's interactive interface accomplished was to evolve bulletin board engagement into a hot, "hypnotic" undertaking. And if there's any question about how hot things can get when people are entranced within a Reddit thread, consider that Reddit may be the most common place on the internet for "flame wars" — long, angry, abusive, and insulting exchanges.

The 2016 US Election and Brexit Referendum (Hot)
Speaking of long, angry, abusive, and insulting exchanges — the heating-up pattern of media through the 2010s reached perhaps peak heat with the 2016 US election and the "Brexit" debate in the United Kingdom.

What deserves attention in these pages about these two referenda is the way in which content was "weaponized" through the hot social channels discussed in the prior pages. Even the cooler alternatives of Twitter and Tumblr were turned hot as channels for the distribution of polarizing positions, putrid conspiracy theories, dangerous disinformation, and outright lies, many conveyed as "memes" using words and images that were honed and tested to create the strongest appeal possible to a populace that had strong emotional investment in the issues at stake in these referenda.

The "weaponization" of content was achieved through three factors. First, the establishment of "farms" of content producers who were paid to write and distribute messages through social media and to support this content as their opinions or fact-based beliefs without actual personal stake in the position or regard for its validity. This created surges of content into the social streams of real users and seemed to validate what they were seeing as important based on the number of people they saw sharing it, which encouraged them to also pass it along — legitimating it further through a "social proof" heuristic. The second unique "weaponization" factor in the 2016 referenda was the emergence of deployment of "bot" social media accounts that further amplified the work of the content farms by appearing to have real people behind them while actually being shell accounts with automated text and attachment posting algorithms.

The third "weaponization" factor in the 2016 referenda was the anonymity that these first two methods gave content publishers while still allowing them to achieve large-scale reach. This anonymity encouraged content creators seeking to drive polarizing views the ability to present any claim they wanted without any chance that they would be directly challenged to defend the position with facts. Put more plainly — it became very easy to lie without ever being challenged, and to have the lie believed and recirculated as truth because it conformed with the receivers pre-existing beliefs, and because it seemed so widely accepted within the receiver's social media ecosystem.

The presence of disinformation and the entrenchment in polarized ideological positioning versus the predominance of facts and interest in reasoned debate over collective interest led to "echo chambers" among those sharing the same predisposition on the issues. Perhaps more detrimentally, when debate could occur among opposing views (perhaps in Facebook), the argument tended to devolve to criticism of the other side's ignorance of the "real" facts, or their emotional support for positions that seemed insurmountable in finding any commonality, and often devolved into flame wars fought with gifs and memes.

While the influence of content farms and bots and the risks from unsubstantiated or untruthful but ideologically resonant claims became apparent through investigations following the 2016 referenda, they are not resolved as issues as of this edition's publication. The solution to the influence of disinformation on populations will likely not be technical or regulatory. Social media networks claim they have begun to look more diligently for bot accounts and disinformation brokers to shut them down when they find them. But the ability to quickly create accounts, spread content, and move on before the monitoring catches up is too easy. Likewise, social media platforms are reluctant to act as the "editorial board" or "fact-checking department" for users of their networks, or to throttle the expression of opinion through their platforms.

Without "fact-checking departments" in these new publishing networks (like those which have existed for all other traditional publishers of print and video), lies will continue to be posted and potentially consumed as fact. The only certain way to ensure that disinformation does not influence large numbers of a population would be the development of a higher level of content literacy and critical thinking in that population that would lead them not to accept their social media stream as a "source" of information until they'd rationally (not ideologically) assessed the fact-checking quality in the origin of the content.

TikTok (Hot/Cool)
This Beijing-founded video sharing technology launched for iOS and Android in 2017. In 2019, the

app — available in over 150 markets and in 75 languages — was listed as the seventh most downloaded mobile app of the 2010s, a position it achieved in just three years of availability.

What made TikTok so hot? For viewers, it offers a stream of instant distraction in the ideal format for mobile consumption. For creators, it limits maximum video length to 60 seconds, and offers easy video and sound editing, an automatic looping function, and a way to interact with other videos through "react" and "duet" formats. Simply, it has provided a fun way for anyone and everyone to create and share snackable video content using just their phone.

You might notice TikTok has been classified here as both hot and cool. This designation is in recognition of the cool nature of the creative process. Bringing forth something from nothing, no matter how easily it is facilitated, requires the maker to create the message from a blank page. Media that facilitates creation offers a cool refuge for the creators — and in turn their ability to create marks them as "cool" among their followers. Thus, a channel that puts cool creative potential into many hands while offering a constant stream of hot content to viewers has to be considered a mix.

As of publication, TikTok's delivery of advertisements is limited, but its content personalization ability is advanced among video sharing networks; using machine learning for content analysis and artificial intelligence for selection to surface videos that are expected to appeal to each user.

The Road Ahead

A trend in the analysis above may have appeared to some readers. It seems that the always-on omnipresent nature of digital media is resulting in a rising average temperature within our overall communications ecosystem.

It is unlikely that new digital formats will ever shift the channels of communication back in a cooler direction. Digital runs hot. Rather, access to cool content by those who need it will be sought through the content's style, based on how much imagination can be brought to involvement with the content. For example, in late 2018, Netflix released an episode of the dystopian series Black Mirror that required the viewer to make choices at pivotal plot moments. Through their choices, viewers receive one from among several endings. Many viewers, on finishing, went back to prior choices to see what outcomes could be achieved if they chose differently. Immersive content that can be "co-created" during consumption will offer some cooler respite from unceasing digital streams.

Cooler escapes will remain in the hotter digital climate; podcasts offer a cool experience akin to radio. Paper books still provide "retro" respite from screens. And the creative side of digital will allow cool creative pursuits to flourish for anyone with access to the creative tools that are moving rapidly into mobile devices. While the results will be distributed through primarily hot media channels, the act of bringing forth something from a blank canvas — via writing, recoding audio, making music, video, coding apps, etc. — is itself engagement in the media at its coolest.

The confluence of digital and physical will also offer cooler opportunities such as 3D printing as a creative exercise, or flying drone-mounted digital cameras as an opportunity to creatively explore one's environment.

Content consumer's needs and motivations will be influenced by the temperature of their cultural environment. Whether their personal world is feeling too hot or too cool will shape the level of interest in consumption of hotter content (hypnosis) or cooler content (hallucination). An ability to anticipate these preferences by understanding the nature of the current communication environment will be essential to digital media planners, communications strategists, experience designers, and the technologists who develop and evolve the channels that deliver these hotter and cooler digital experiences.

10.2 Organizational Change for Effective Digital Analytics

A deep understanding of the influence that content has on culture (and the consumers in it) is a requirement for companies that wish to thrive. However, the ability for companies to act on this understanding is equally important. Without the ability to act, consumer insights are just useless trivia.

In the effort to turn analytics into action, it is important that companies understand that becoming data-driven is a process of change, and that change is often difficult. Change is difficult because it takes individuals and organizations into the unknown — it requires new thinking and new behavior — and for most people it is easier and more comfortable to keep doing what they already know how to do than to learn new ways of thinking and acting.

In fact, our brains actually seek ways to reduce the amount of information we need to consciously process in our day-to-day environment. By routinizing the "little things" and limiting the intrusion of unimportant stimuli in our day-to-day activity, we leave more processing power for those things we deem important. Or at least that's the idea.

The automatic psychological tactics our brains apply to recognize the stuff that happens regularly in our lives and filter it out of conscious processing is the "familiarity heuristic". Look around you (or at you) at school or work and you'll see people "going through the motions" without seeming to think their way through the routine. Two other common heuristics tend to create challenges for organizational change. The first is a heuristic known as "social proof", which is the tendency for individuals to conform to the activity they observe from others in a group, particularly when confronted with ambiguity or uncertainty. This can also be thought of as pack or herd behavior. The second is a bias or heuristic called "escalation of commitment". This interesting bias results in people justifying an increasing level of commitment to prior decisions even when confronted with new evidence that indicates that abandonment of the current course of action and development of a new approach would be more productive.

When the familiarity, social proof, and escalation of commitment heuristics operate together in organizations, we find places where managers are reflexively invested in maintaining the routines and methods and processes that got them into management, but which might not help the enterprise moving forward (such as shifting some of the decision-making influence from experience to analysis). Strategies and tactics that should be reexamined based on changes in the business situation fall within organizational structures that should also be reexamined. The example of the "go fever" that gripped NASA in advance of the Challenger launch is a tragic example of the danger these biases can cause for organizations.

Systems Thinking

Tackling the biases and heuristics which limit the capability for change within organizations requires explicit organizational change strategy. Some of the best recent thinking on organizational change has come from MIT. This is not surprising because MIT is a driver of technological innovation, and the successful adoption of any innovation requires a change from an old way of acting (without the technology) to a new way of acting (with the technology). One of the leading thinkers at MIT is Peter Senge, who first became known in the area of organizational development with the publication of a book titled *The Fifth Discipline* in which he introduced the idea of a learning organization; a company that puts learning and change at its core to ensure ongoing transformation and growth.

At the center of the learning organization is the cultivation of "systems thinking". Systems thinking is the ability for an individual to unravel the context of their environment, or the "system" in which they operate, into a series of separate threads that collectively form the system. One thread people may consciously discover and account for is how their own patterns of thought and activity translate from seemingly insignificant day-to-day attitudes and actions into a component part of the organization and how it works, and as such how, from the inside out, they actually create the forces which they may have previously perceived of as an impersonal organization acting on them from the outside in.

Systems thinking can be summarized well with the questions "Why are we doing this, and what could we being doing differently?" As Senge puts it, "The fundamental rationale of systems thinking is to understand how it is that the problems that we all deal with which are the most vexing, difficult, and intransigent come about, and to give us some perspective on those problems [in order to] give us some leverage and insight as to what we might do differently".

Senge outlines the benefit of systems thinking as providing organizations with "the ability to discern non-obvious areas of high leverage", or in other words, to develop competitive advantage through the ability to create and act upon change. As Senge puts it in a 2011 interview produced by IBM, "... when you ask, what does it take, in a business context, for people to start to discern non-obvious areas of leverage, the answer is, a very deep and persistent commitment to learning. There are a couple of features to this commitment to learning. One is, I have to be prepared to be wrong. Again, if it was pretty obvious what needed to be done, we'd already be doing it. So, I'm part of the problem...my own way of seeing things, my own sense of where there's leverage, is probably part of the problem. This is the domain we've always called 'mental models'. If I'm not prepared to challenge my own mental models, the likelihood of finding non-obvious areas of high leverage is low".

The purpose of analysis is to identify patterns and provide explanations for those patterns in ways that inform actions to optimize desired outcomes. These patterns have more value when they provide unexpected insight, or in Senge's terms, when they provide "non-obvious areas of high leverage". Of course, finding these unique insights will not happen until we begin to understand how our pre-existing mental models, biases, or heuristics are limiting our perspective, and until we recognize that we ourselves need to change for the system to change. Nowhere is this truer than for managers in a business that is looking to become more data-driven. In such an environment looking to undergo organizational change, not only is the manager challenged in the implied shift of their role from "answer definer" to "question asker", but they will also be tasked with guiding the organization's ability to find "non-obvious sources of high leverage" in the data, and to apply these to achieve results. Engendering systems thinking is the place to start. For an understanding of how to begin this process, we turn to a second MIT professor — Otto Scharmer, a Senior Lecturer at Sloan School of Business and co-founder of the Presencing Institute, the origin of "Theory U".

Theory U

> *The success of an intervention depends on the interior condition of the intervener.*
>
> — Bill O'Brien, CEO, Hanover Insurance

The quote above is provided within Professor Scharmer's book *Theory U: Leading from the Future as it Emerges,* and perfectly summarizes his underlying message. Scharmer shares Senge's view of environments in need of change as systems that have been built and maintained by the very people who need to make the changes, and the related importance of each individual's recognition of their role in (re) structuring the systems of which they are a part. The underlying principle of Scharmer's "Theory U" is that positive change can only emerge when individuals stop "downloading" from the existing system and instead begin to use new information and creativity to start bringing the best possible future into the present, a process he calls "Presencing". This concept of "Presencing" is grounded partly in the requirement captured in the quotation that starts this system; the requirement that individuals who hope to intervene for good in their systems must be consciously present within those systems to take the first step away from the default state of "downloading", which can also be thought of as acting reflexively from the "familiarity", "social proof", and "escalation of commitment" heuristics described earlier in this chapter.

Recognizing and addressing the heuristics, filters, and biases that shape the perspective of each of us as individuals in our environment is a key first step to enacting the type of change that will transform our organization to be more "data-driven" and able to act on unexpected insights. Scharmer's "Theory U" also provides a nicely structured understanding of the organization, and the "organizational life" of individuals that provides context around the manifestation of our collective internal conditions into the external conditions we perceive as a system.

Scharmer outlines three "layers" of organizational life that collectively compose what we think of as the "system" in an organization:

1. **Objective Structures:** This is the dimension of the organization as defined by the "Org Chart" and structured through established tools and processes.
2. **Enacted Structures:** This is the dimension of the organization defined by informal social networks. While the objective organization dictates "who is in charge of what", the enacted structure tends to determine how things actually get done. This structure is where "who you know" matters more than your position in an org chart, and "what you know" matters more than your defined job function.
3. **Personal Sources of Enactment:** This is the foundation of the organization, and the source of all activity in the enacted structures and systems described above. This is the position from which each individual in the organization takes action, and is defined by the collective perspectives, attitudes, biases, and filters of each individual in the organization. When filters and biases are high, perspectives are narrow, attitudes lack energy and positivity, and the organization will be inflexible and resistant to the change it will sorely need.

Because so much activity inside organizations is guided by heuristics and processed through filters, any proposed change that might result in a need to leave this comfort zone will be perceived as a threat unless (1) it is offered with context that links the change required by each individual to a bigger picture vision of an organizational outcome, and (2) solves something that these individuals agree needs to be solved.

The "U" in Scharmer's "Theory U" is essentially a "U-turn" for individuals and the way they work within and perceive their organizations. The shape reflects a process of "diving-down" to a point of deep understanding of oneself and one's role in generating the present of the organization, then building back up on the other side of this process to ultimately act as the embodiment of a new and better way of organizational work. On the left, or downward sloping side of the "U", there are four stages in shifting from the current state to a place of readiness for change.

The default state of organizational awareness is *Downloading/Conforming*. Here the individual speaks from what is expected/learned. This is clearly the antithesis of an analytical and data-driven mindset and environment. True analysts will not do well in this environment, and data or analysis that contradicts the established conformity will be rejected without reason.

The first level of awareness deepening is to *Debate/ Confronting*. Here the individual begins speaking from what they think. While this type of awareness is at least capable of diverging from other views, for each individual acting from this position, it is very unidirectional and defensive; their thinking and perspective flows out into the organization, but little is let back in to shape or transform their beliefs. Heuristics and biases still rule the day in this world, they are simply less shared. An analyst who can only present what they think and cannot hear other perspectives will be limited in the value of insight they can deliver. A manager who thinks this way will use data when it supports their position, and reject data when it does not.

The next level of awareness is one of *Dialogue/ Relating.* Here the individual understands that they are part of a system, and speaks from the standpoint of seeing themselves as part of the whole. This is clearly a much more productive position for all involved. Analysis produced from this perspective will be cognizant of the needs of others and the system as a whole, and as such will be more valuable to all. Managers who work from this perspective tend to be focused more on enabling the best options even if they come from others versus constraining activity to only those ideas which come from them. In this environment, data and models that point out a better direction will be accepted and utilized.

The deepest level of awareness is *Presencing/ Connecting.* Here the individual is not afraid to speak from what can emerge, and to enable and join a flow of ideas and creativity across the organization. Analysts who can work from this position will regularly produce insights that are welcomed as perceptive, creative, and able to help drive innovation and progress in the organization. Managers who work from this perspective are allowing their organizations to create a sum that is greater than its parts. Data and models are welcomed if they resolve the need to spend energy and effort on something that is just as easily or better managed algorithmically, and accordingly free up the organization's thinking for more creative pursuits.

When a critical mass of influential individuals in an organization have collectively reached the presencing level of awareness, the organization is certainly ready to become "data-driven", and to make the most of that readiness in terms of quickly developing creative responses to the "non-obvious sources of high leverage" that a readiness for continuous discovery enables. But not all organizations have achieved a level of dialogue or presencing that makes them ready to go where the data tells them to go. So how can a reader of this book begin to initiate change in their own perspective, and then in their organization, to become able to find and apply insights from data?

Leadership and Change

In his book *Leading at the Speed of Change*, Daryl Connor defines the roles that people in organizations will take around any sort of organizational change. As explored above, there will typically be a large contingent who are initially resistant to change. When it comes to change related to data and the transformation to more data-driven practice, the likely first line of resistance will come from the "Targets" of change, the managers who are responsible for the current system of data utilization, and the teams that are accustomed to doing their daily work within that system. This latter group is also the first group that is likely to spawn advocates for change as the benefits of the potential change are defined, and those individuals capable of dialogue and presencing begin to envision a better system as a result of the change.

As Connor has observed, there are typically three other roles working to enact the change for the "Targets" of change. "Sponsors" are the formal leaders in the organization who provide political capital and resources in support of the change effort. These are the individuals who can use organizational authority to mandate that the change should happen. However, even with the contribution of mandate, time and budget, as systems are organic products of the individuals within them, mandates do not become enacted simply based on their presentation by the organizations formal leadership. As Scharmer observed, there is an "enacted" system in organizations underlying the formal structure with a set of relationships and informal processes that determine how things actually get done.

The role emerging from this "enacted" organizational structure is the "Advocate" for change. Even with strong sponsorship within the formal system of an organization, a change effort without Advocates in the enacted layer is sentenced to failure. While formal authority provided by sponsors in leadership is critical for enacting change, support for change provided by advocates who fall within the Target population that will be most affected by the change is perhaps the most powerful form of advocacy for getting the idea for change off the ground and into practice. People in organizations understand that they have to follow the letter of the law as dictated by the Objective structure, but without belief in the spirit of the law, this typically translates into going through the motions around a new "process" that is viewed as an imposition, and is eventually abandoned due to a lack of results. Advocates for change are those who believe in the spirit of the vision for change that underlies a managerial mandate, and who are able, through dialogue and presencing, to translate that vision into terms that can be appreciated by their peers.

The role that draws most heavily from the practices of "presencing" to bring the future into the present through organizational change is the "Change Agent". Many of you reading this far into this chapter will be interested in taking on this role in an effort to help your organization begin utilizing some of the approaches to Digital Analytics outlined in this book, and hopefully the discussion in this chapter has provided you with guidance into how this may be accomplished. As you seek to implement change, ensure you have Sponsorship, recognize your Targets, develop Advocates, and cultivate those Advocates into other Change Agents. Use the ideas defined by Senge to shed light on the system, defining the problems of the system that most need to be addressed, and using data to find "non-obvious sources of high leverage" that can be used to address them. And use the ideas defined by Scharmer to establish a position of presencing in your "personal field of enactment" to place the most creative power behind your effort to drive change, and to draw others as Advocates and supporting Change Agents into your cause.

Overcoming Organizational Inertia

We will end this chapter with some guidance on specific strategic and tactical considerations to make in efforts to build a more data-driven organization. These questions return us to the "Data Applied" section of the ACAP, and may be asked and answered as a preface to that section. In auditing the organization to prepare for change to a more data-driven structure, ask the following questions:

- What data are used in the design and delivery of digital experiences?
- What data are used in the evaluation and optimization of digital performance?
- Where is communication design work being done from guesses or by rote process?
- Are there data available that should be used but aren't?
- Are there design or performance questions that need data that are not available?
- Is performance viewed in business silos versus integrated across channel, like the customer experience?

As a "Change Agent" fueled with the creative power of a "presencing" mindset, seek to expand your new mindset to others. Through the Development of the ACAP, you will have made a giant step toward change by defining a data-analytics strategy that can become a part of collective dialogue. To see the change through, ensure that Sponsors, Advocates, and Targets — even initial resistors to change — have all contributed to the dialogue (which in the case of resistors will have been debate initially, but can become dialogue as they are engaged in that way).

Finally, return to the principles for valuable analysis and visualization to ensure you are building front-line capabilities that actually deliver the results that have been envisioned through the process of change. While sophisticated analytics solutions will create opportunities to identify non-obvious areas of high leverage, these solutions must manifest in interfaces and visualizations that are so simple and useful that managers and employees will want to use them daily. As you implement analytics, do not allow the effort and investment to be so heavily weighted toward models that frontline usage gets overlooked, since models and analytics are only truly valuable to the business when they can be used to drive positive results for the business and the consumer alike.

Conclusion

Thank you for taking the time to read and learn more about digital analytics and conversion science. If this book has done its job, then the preceding pages have answered that key question facing you as a marketer: "how do I deliver content and experience around my brand that is relevant enough to drive engagement in the user's current context?"

Ideally, these chapters have helped guide you to ideas for good answers to this question through a foundation in marketing and consumer behavior theory, an understanding of marketing methods with a conversion focus, and insights into the technical, cultural, and organizational concerns that can drive or hinder advancement of data-driven consumer experience.

Although you have reached the end of this book, you are still on the path of what will undoubtedly turn out to be a long and interesting journey working with communications to shape consumer behavior. As you follow the path that proceeds from these pages into your own next chapter, please stay connected via this book's counterpart website (www. architectingexperience.com) for access to supporting material (e.g. the ACAP template), expanded thinking around this book, and the opportunity to share your experiences and ideas with peers and colleagues.

Index

A

A/B/n testing, 175
above the line, 125
acquisition, 190
active evaluation, 40–41
Acxiom, 54, 80
adaptive analytics, 70
addressable TV, 132
ad network, 50, 133
ad supported, 6
Ad Tech, 137
advertising, 7, 117, 121, 129
advertising exchange, 133
aided awareness, 186
Alexa, 159
algorithmic recommendations, 15
algorithms, 57
Amazon Go, 169
analysis, 45, 196
anonymized, 213
application programming interface (API), 125, 204
app permissions, 209
apps, 167

ARIMA, 217
attention, 14, 33, 41, 97–99, 103, 115, 118
attention capture, 5
attribution, 188, 192, 194–195
audience, 7, 19
audience metrics, 190
augmented reality (AR), 147, 168, 240
authoritarianism, 110
awareness, 94, 104, 131, 186

B

behavioral segmentation, 53
behavioral targeting, 41
behavior metrics, 190
below the line, 125, 131
biases, 252
big data, 58
Bit Torrent, 230
Black Mirror, 246
Blogosphere, 229
bots, 244
bounce rate, 191

brand awareness, 134
brand consideration, 134
branded content, 119,
150–151
branding, 28
brand tracking surveys,
186
broadband/high-speed,
228
business objective, 73–74
business problem
statement, 72
business to business
(B2B), 26
business to consumer
(B2C), 26

C
cable, 14
California Consumer
Privacy Act (CCPA),
211–212, 214
call-to-action (CTA), 66,
118, 131
Cambridge Analytica,
210–212, 214
capitalism, 110
Cartesian Theater, 105
challenger space shuttle,
198
Christenson, Clayton, 36
classification, 81
Classification and
Regression Trees
(CART) analysis, 217
click bait, 103
clickstream aggregators,
53
click-through, 50

click-through rate, 187,
189
closure, 103
cloud storage, 60
cognition, 104
cognitive tedium, 122
Connor, Daryl, 256–257
consciousness, 104–107
consideration, 128
consideration set, 40
consumer behavior, 32,
42, 111
consumer-centered
strategy, 74
consumer data vendors,
54
consumer decision
journey, 38–39, 41, 92
consumer insights, 22
consumer journey, 118,
126–127, 216
consumer packaged goods
(CPG) companies, 48
consumption, 114
content, 2–5, 17
content farms, 244
content literacy, 244
content marketing, 151
content optimization, 41
content product, 117
content ranking
algorithms, 154
contextual analytics, 63
contextual insights, 64
conversion, 4, 25, 42, 72,
111, 118, 128, 184, 190
conversion data, 48–49
conversion metrics, 192
conversion science, 52

cool media, 226
cool medium, 234
correlation, 64, 81, 84
cost per acquisition
 (CPA), 192
cost per click (CPC),
 187–188
CPM, 185
creative agencies, 9, 19
creative platform, 97
critical thinking, 244
CTR, 188
cultural capital, 3
cultural narratives,
 110–111, 113
cultural norms, 113
culture, 13, 109, 247
customer data platform
 (CDP), 55, 137, 140,
 207–208
customer experience
 (CX), 18
customer insights, 20
customer profile, 206–207
Customer Relationship
 Management (CRM),
 41, 51, 89, 125, 140,
 142, 208
customer service, 41

D
3D printing, 247
dark patterns, 164–165
darkpatterns.org, 165
dashboards, 63, 189
data, 7, 45
data applications pyramid,
 61
data collection, 46

data-driven, 247
data-driven organization,
 259
data management
 platform (DMP),
 137–139, 208
data requirements, 61
data syndication services,
 48
data transformation, 205
Dawkins, Richard, 232
decision tree, 217
deductive analysis, 77, 79
deductive approach, 78
demand-side platform
 (DSP), 66, 137–138,
 209
democracy, 110
demographic metrics, 190
Dennett, Daniel, 105
Descartes, René, 104
descriptive analytics, 62
descriptive statistics, 64
design, 74
digital advertising, 9
digital analytics, 47
digital content, 125
digital distribution, 5–6
digital literacy, 237
digital natives, 233, 236
digital publishing, 5
digital search, 50
digital streaming, 133
digital targeting, 133
direct marketing, 126
direct to consumer
 (D2C), 11, 18, 48, 56
disinformation, 243–244
"dot-com" bubble, 229

E
echo chambers, 243
ecology, 111
e-commerce, 19
economics, 111
efficiency, 135, 192
email, 125, 189, 228
email marketing, 144–145
emergence, 99
emotion, 119–120
engagement, 14, 116
entertainment, 27, 116
environmental impact, 114
escalation of commitment, 248
ethics, 113, 215
ETL, 206
Experian, 54
experience, 4, 6, 14, 18
experience barrier, 177
experience design, 58, 173
experience driver, 177
experience map, 92–93, 126, 141–142
experiment, 177
experimentation, 174, 184

F
Facebook, 137, 209–212, 230, 235, 243
facial recognition, 214
fact-checking, 244
factor analysis, 83–84
factual, 53
familiarity heuristic, 248
file transfer, 204
filters, 252
first party data, 52

flame wars, 242–243
forecasting, 66
frequency, 185
Friendster, 230

G
General Data Protection Regulation (GDPR), 211–212
Gen X, 235
Gestalt, 99–102, 104
goals, 192
going viral, 231
Google Assistant, 159
Google Glass, 239
gradient decent, 224
gradient descent, 219, 223
gross rating points (GRPs), 185
growth, 30, 32

H
hashtag, 234
health impact, 114
heuristics, 100, 252
hipster, 236
Hipsterism, 233
hot and cold media, 13, 225, 227
hot media, 226
HTML, 228
Hulu, 240
human–computer interaction (HCI), 17
humor, 120
hypotheses, 65, 175
hypothesis, 77, 174, 176–177, 179

I

identity graphs, 55
immersive content, 246
impressions, 50, 185
incremental sales, 182
inductive analysis, 77, 79–80
influencer marketing, 9
information, 45
in-game advertising, 146
insights, 197
Instagram, 137
integrated data repository, 205
interfaces, 16
internet, 227
invariance, 100
iPad, 237, 239
iPhone, 232

J

jobs to be done (JTBD), 35–37, 43, 76, 78, 90, 97, 115, 126, 128

K

Kahneman, Daniel, 33
key performance indicator (KPI), 62, 72, 164, 176, 184
keywords, 155
Kindle, 237
K-means clustering, 77, 81

L

landing page, 161
Last.fm, 238–239
law of double jeopardy, 31

leads, 134
LEGO, 151
life events, 39–40
linear regression, 85, 216
location, 213–214
location-based, 235
location-based targeting, 146
location intelligence, 53
Locke, John, 104
logistic regression, 217
look-alike audiences, 134
look-alike modeling, 53
look-alike models, 183
lower funnel, 12
loyalty loop, 42

M

machine leaning, 217, 223–224
machine learning algorithms, 70
manufacturers, 48
marketing, 28
marketing automation (MA), 140, 184, 189
marketing automation software, 66
marketing research, 64
marketing technology, 11
market insights, 22
mass marketing, 129
mass media, 2, 50
mass reach, 125
McLuhan, Marshall, 12, 112, 225–227, 229, 233, 240
measurement, 94
media, 12, 112

media agencies, 9, 11, 19
media strategy, 117,
    127–128
media targeting, 55
meme, 232
mental availability, 30, 32,
    35, 40–41, 43, 119, 151,
    186
micro-blogging, 236
millenials, 233
MIT, 249
mobile, 4, 235
mobile advertising, 146
mobile games, 146
motivations, 21
Mozilla browser, 228
multi-stability, 100
multivariate regression, 85
multivariate testing
    (MVT), 175
MySpace, 230

N
Napster, 230
Netflix, 240
neural network, 219,
    221–224
news, 27

O
objectives, 19, 134
Oculus Rift, 239
online retail, 26
open rate, 189
optimization analytics, 65
opt-in, 51
organic social media
    marketing, 158

organizational change, 248
organizational silos, 46
out of home (OOH), 8,
    129
over the top (OTT), 132
owned experience, 50

P
Pandora, 238–239
path analysis, 63
path to purchase, 10
paywall, 15
peer referral, 158
peer-to-peer file-sharing,
    230
perception, 8, 99
performance, 177
performance analytics, 20,
    62–64
performance KPIs, 187
performance
    measurement, 184
personally identifiable
    information, 80, 211,
    213–214
personally identifying
    information, 54
physical availability, 30, 32
Pinterest, 237
PlaceIQ, 53
political structure, 111
positive habituation, 122
predictions, 215–216
predictive analytics, 67,
    190
predictive models, 66
prescriptive analytics, 69,
    218–219

print, 129
programmatic, 66
programmatic targeting, 135, 181
propensity, 195
publishers, 19
purchase funnel, 38

Q
qualitative research, 47, 86–89

R
radio, 129
random forest, 218
reach, 121, 125, 128–130, 134–135, 185
real-time bidding (RTB), 135
Red Bull, 51
Reddit, 241
regression, 86
reification, 100, 103
relevance, 14–15, 137
repetition, 121–122
research, 21, 68, 75
resonance, 118
responsibility, 111, 114
Return on Ad Spend (ROAS), 182
return on advertising investment, 50
return on investment (ROI), 49, 66, 94
return on marketing, 49
return on marketing investment (ROMI), 50, 193

S
sales, 23, 134
salience, 116
sample size, 180
Scharmer, Otto, 251–253
Schultz, Don, 236
search engine, 155
search engine marketing (SEM), 9, 126, 157
search engine optimization (SEO), 126, 154
segmentation, 63–64
segments, 23, 77, 90, 180, 211
self, 108
self-interest, 110
Senge, Peter, 249–251, 258
Sharp, Byron, 29
shopper marketing, 168
similarity, 102
similar Web, 53
Siri, 159
Snapchat, 238
Snow, John, 201
socialism, 110
social media, 5, 158
social media marketing, 9
social networks, 125, 136, 227, 230
social proof, 248
sound and music, 103
SoundCloud, 239
South by Southwest, 234
Spotify, 238–239
Stasko, John, 196
statistical confidence, 88

statistical significance,
    176, 180
strategy and planning, 75
streaming data, 57
structured data, 58
sub-consciousness, 104
sub-culture, 232
subscription, 6–7, 15, 25
Superbowl, 116
supervised, 217
survey questionnaire, 88
suspense, 120
symmetry, 102
System 1, 34, 43
System 2, 34
systems thinking, 249–250

T
tactical plan, 128
targeting, 53, 137, 180,
    182
target rating points
    (TRPs), 185
task-distracting, 116
task-distraction, 145
task-relevance, 116–117
technographic variables,
    190
television, 129, 227
test, 177
test goals, 176
testing, 65, 68, 174–175,
    183–184
text messages, 229
textual literacy, 237
the medium is the
    message, 226
theory, 77

Theory U, 251–252, 254
Thinking Fast and Slow, 33
thinking fast/system 1, 99
third party data, 53
third party data providers,
    54
TikTok, 245
time-series, 217
totalitarianism, 110
traditional advertising,
    125
traffic, 134
triggers, 39
Tumblr, 235–236
Twitch, 241
Twitter, 233–235

U
unaided awareness, 186
Unilever, 51–52, 55, 58
unstructured data, 59
unsupervised, 217
user experience (UX), 6,
    14, 74, 161–162, 215
user-generated content, 7
user interface (UI), 6, 161
UX design, 76

V
variety, 46–47
velocity, 46, 57
video content, 125
video formats, 131
video on demand (VOD),
    132
view-through rate,
    187–188
virtual machines, 60

virtual reality (VR), 148,
239
visual design, 102
visualization, 196–197,
199
vlogging, 231
voice search, 159
volume, 46, 58–59

W

weaponization of content,
242–243
websites, 155, 161
wholesalers, 48

Y

YouTube, 231–232

CPSIA information can be obtained
at www.ICGtesting.com
Printed in the USA
BVHW041413060820
585641BV00004B/13